BEING YOU,
CHANGING THE
WORLD

(IS NOW THE TIME?)

BEING YOU, CHANGING THE WORLD

(IS NOW THE TIME?)

BY DR. DAIN HEER

ACCESS
CONSCIOUSNESS®
PUBLISHING

Being You, Changing the World
Copyright © 2015 by Dr. Dain C. Heer

ISBN: 978-1-939261-02-1
Hardcover ISBN: 978-1-63493-022-2

Editor: Katarina Wallentin
Cover design: Katarina Wallentin
Cover photo: Allannah Avelin
Interior design: Toni Burton

Published by Access Consciousness Publishing, LLC

www.accessconsciousnesspublishing.com

Printed in the United States of America
2nd Edition

First Edition, copyright © 2012 by Dr. Dain C. Heer, published by Big Country Publishing, LLC

"You may say I'm a dreamer, but I'm not the only one.
I hope some day you'll join us...and the world will be as one."
—John Lennon

"Be the change you want to see in the world."
—Mahatma Gandhi

"Be You and Change the World."
—Gary M. Douglas

What some people say about this book...

"You rocked my world with this book. I'm observing magical things. I AM AWARE that every single aspect of my life is transforming ... I am 62, and really cannot remember a time in my life when I was not aware of and seeking what you talk about, in one way or another. Yes, this is the time for me. In all the experiences I have had the privilege of having, this seems to be the icing on the cake. I am just so very grateful."

- Ann

"Thank you so much for having written this book ... EVERYTHING you say resonated with lightness in my heart and for the first time in my life I feel that somebody understands me. My sense of my value has changed within the last 52 minutes while you were reading your first chapter. I cannot thank you enough...."

- Stefanie

"I am very grateful for you and for your new book. I bought if for my son and he had some challenging times in his life. (He has ADD, took Ritalin for a year, became a 'zombie' and didn't want to live anymore, dropped out of school and didn't seem to fit in any system.) He totally adored your book; he read it in one night. He told me he suddenly understood lots of things in his life. He even bought some drawing stuff and started drawing again."

- Caro

"Thank you so much for writing this book and for doing it in the format you have. I have found it to be my best friend when I can't seem to get clear on multiple occasions and it is wonderful to see where I can use it to empower myself to live with more ease, joy and glory. I'm intensely grateful that you were courageous enough to do it YOUR way. It truly works for me. Without all the separations and small paragraphs, it would be nearly impossible for me to use it as the "Magical Book of Pragmatic Transformational Wisdom for Today" that it truly is."

- Jason

"This was only chapter one and you had me giggling like a little girl, crying tears of letting go, joy and remembering who I truly am."

- Cheryle

GRATITUDE

When you have so many phenomenal people in your life, it is not easy to express the gratitude you have for them in just one page.

I'd like to start by thanking Gary Douglas, the founder of Access Consciousness®. How do you thank someone for not only saving your life but giving you the tools to create a completely new one? He empowers everyone he meets to truly choose for themselves. How did the world get so lucky?

I'd also like to thank the editor and co-creator of this book, Katarina Wallentin. Without her tireless effort, this book would never have come into existence. Her ability to take a seemingly-endless series of transcripts from Energetic Synthesis of Being (ESB) classes and coax them into an initial manuscript is a Herculean effort that she made seem almost effortless. (Also, working with me can't be easy, but she sure made it seem as though it was.)

I'd also like to thank all of the participants of Access Consciousness classes and Energetic Synthesis of Being classes, who together have been willing to go where no man, woman, or child has gone before, and without whom much of the material in this book would not be.

I'd like to thank my Mom, who has always allowed me to be as weird and as much of a "dreamer" as I am, no matter what that looked like. I can't overstate what a gift that level of allowance for me and my choices has been in my life.

Thank you also to the Access Consciousness crew—the staff—and the many talented Access facilitators throughout the world, who are contributing to creating a world with greater possibilities for us all. Lastly, but definitely not least, thank YOU—for being someone who desires something greater and is willing to choose it. Together, I know we can create a world greater than any of us can currently imagine.

CONTENTS

Tools:

Beautiful You,

Somehow this book ended up in your hands.
How does it get even better than that?

So is now the time?
Are you willing to be you and change the world?

If so, my courageous friend, before you start reading,
say this out loud, all five times.

Yes, out loud.

Everything is the opposite of what it appears to be.
Nothing is the opposite of what it appears to be.

Everything is the opposite of what it appears to be.
Nothing is the opposite of what it appears to be.

Everything is the opposite of what it appears to be.
Nothing is the opposite of what it appears to be.

Everything is the opposite of what it appears to be.
Nothing is the opposite of what it appears to be.

Everything is the opposite of what it appears to be.
Nothing is the opposite of what it appears to be.

Now you are sufficiently prepared. Turn the page and begin the journey
into **weirdness**.

─── INTRODUCTION ───

I didn't write this book for everyone. I wrote it for the few—the people that realize that this reality in its current form is not working to bring about the greater "us" that is truly possible. I wrote it for the "dreamers"—those that know that something different—and greater—should be possible, and that we should be able to have it.

You "dreamers" are my people. You are the ones who can truly change the world, if you can just allow yourself the permission to do it. If you can come out of the idea that this reality—as it is—will ever be enough for you. And if you can simply begin to realize that EVERY LIMITATION you've ever thought you had was simply a greatness that you couldn't yet recognize.

If you were being you—who would you be?

What if you, truly Being you, is all it takes to change EVERYTHING — your life, everyone around you and the world? What if you, being you, were the missing key to having everything you've ever desired or wanted to create and change in the world? What if you being you meant receiving everything, being everything, knowing everything and perceiving EVERYTHING?

Do you know that it's time to "wake up"? That's what this book is meant to do. It isn't like any other self-improvement book you've ever read. It's not the same old spiritual/psychological re-hash of the same old stuff, with different words. It's not the kind of book that you read and then judge yourself for being inadequate afterwards. No, this is a book about empowering you to change many of the ways in which you are judging you, making you wrong, and feeling inadequate.

It is about coming out of the judgment of you and the idea that you are wrong in any way. Maybe it will even invite you to know that more is possible. Imagine what it would be like ... to not have to feel wrong about you in any way, for any reason, ever again.

What if you are the difference the earth requires? Is now the time to step up?

So what does it take to truly be you? Would you be willing to try something completely different?

It isn't about succeeding as you. Or doing something better. It is about BEING you, being the ENERGY of you, whatever that may be.

Has anyone ever asked you to show up as you? Just you, exactly as you are?

I'd like to invite you to this: being the energy of you.

Start by reading and USING the tools in this book. They may seem really simple, but please don't discount them because of that. If you choose to use these tools, your life will change—and your investment in this book will be worth many times whatever you paid for it.

You don't even have to put massive amounts of work into the exercises in this book. Reading them is all that's required—and the willingness to change. Just the willingness. You don't have to know how the change is going to occur. The "how" is up to the Universe. Use the tools and allow the Universe to work for you.

If you could figure out your life by thinking, if you could mentally figure out how to be you, wouldn't you have done so already? If thinking yourself out of the box actually worked—wouldn't you be generating a totally different reality by now? I mean, really, haven't you been trying to think your way out of the box forever?

If you are willing, this book can give you an awareness and a reminder of what it is like to BE YOU, beyond the cognitive, and beyond the logical mind. It also gives you the tools to choose YOU.

Throughout this book, I'll be asking you to look at things from a different perspective. Why? Because looking at things from the same perspective has created the life you currently have. If that were enough for you, you wouldn't be reading this book.

Would you be willing to find out who you truly be?
Would you be willing to make the demand that you show up?
Would you be willing to know what's really true for YOU?

Let me tell you a bit about the playing field. . . .

Part I of the book is about the things that stop you from being you. This is where we'll explore the limitations of the box you call your life—that don't have to be! I will show you some key areas where you may have been buying a lot of things as true for you that are not. We will look deeply at this reality, the cancer called judgment (and how it stops us and kills us in ways you may never have imagined), receiving, caring, relationships, love, family, abuse and your body.

You will also be introduced to some of the tools that can assist you in changing all of this. What else is possible if everything this reality considers important and valuable . . . is an illusion? And not truly important and valuable FOR YOU?

In Part II, we will explore what is beyond all that . . . What are the INFINITE possibilities? What if you are magic? What if you were the leader of your life? What if we lived in the Kingdom of We instead of walling ourselves off in the artificially created Kingdom of Me? What if the Earth didn't need saving? And . . . what if you being you is the gift that is required to change the world?

Along the way, I'll give you many things to ponder. I will offer you the possibility of changing many things NOW. Please know, it is always your choice. And as long as you are choosing, I have no point of view about what you choose. Please, just keep choosing. For you. For all of us.

We, especially us "dreamers," seem to spend an inordinate amount of time trying to fix what we feel must be wrong with us, rather than creating and generating a different world—a world with the kind of possibilities we'd like to be able to choose. As we explore many of the ways in which you may have been keeping yourself stuck, I'll point out some completely different possibilities and different ways of looking at things that you may never have considered before—and many that you probably have considered, but didn't know that you could choose or institute.

And always with the invitation, "Would you like to choose something different here?" Because even when you don't know how that different reality is going to get created, your choice is always the first step to getting there.

You don't have to know "how" that choice is going to show up. Your choice that it shows up, changes the world to begin to allow it to happen. The Universe's job is fulfillment. You just have to choose to move in that direction—and just keep moving. If you do, no one and nothing will ever stop you again.

As the title suggests, this book is written from the awareness that you, being you, will truly change not only your life, but also the world. In fact, incredible people being willing to be them and choose according to what they know— no matter the criticism, or the judgment or anyone else's point of view—is the only thing that ever has changed the world.

This is not a book of answers!
I am not a guru.
I am not perfect, and I don't have any answers for you.
I only have questions.

This book is about possibilities—the possibility for a completely different way of being in the world.

Way back in 2000, I made a demand that changed my life. For my whole life I was one of those dreamers. I did everything I could to make others around me happy. I did everything I could think of to contribute to making people's lives a better place. I went to chiropractic college so I could learn new and better ways of creating "miracles" in people's bodies and lives, because I KNEW IT SHOULD BE POSSIBLE.

Yet, this reality, and the problems of this reality, weighed so heavily on me that I became hopeless that it would ever change. I had most of the things that were supposed to matter here, but very little of it did.

I began to wake up depressed and unhappy, unbeknownst to my family at the time. I began hating to go to my practice because I felt like nothing I did was enough. It was like people didn't have the tools they required to truly create change in their lives. Worse yet, I felt like I was the only one that wanted something truly different as a reality. No one seemed to "get" me, and to be the only one of my kind was almost unbearable.

Then, by total surprise to me, I found a way out … a way beyond … a way to change everything that I thought could not be changed. And I was given access to my life again, access to a desire to LIVE, and to fully enjoy it, to know that I was a contribution, and to KNOW that there was something else possible—and most importantly—to know that everything I always thought was true actually is.

To the best of my ability, this is what I'll be sharing with you as we explore Being You, Changing The World.

Why ME?
Why did I write this book?

In 2000, when I came to that point in my life where I had enough of this reality, I had everything anyone could ask for—yet nothing of that had any value to me.

I was willing to end it all if things didn't change. Deep down I knew something different was possible. I knew.

Like you do.

I made a demand of the Universe: Either my life completely changes or I am out of here. I even set a date, 6 months in the future. I gave the Universe a deadline. Literally a week later, I found something that changed my entire life: Access Consciousness ("Access" for short). During my first session, I experienced a sense and awareness of being peace and space that I had been looking for all my life, and I never contemplated killing myself again. And I hope, with this book, that I can give you that gift also. Since then, the peace and space has just continued to GROW, in contrast to every other modality I had ever tried.

The tools I am sharing with you in this book are part of Access—and they have continued to expand my living and my consciousness every moment of every day from my first contact with them.

Access is the weirdest, wildest, wackiest modality I have ever come across—and it works. It just works.

One way of describing Access is as an energy transformation modality which links seasoned wisdom, ancient knowledge and highly contemporary, pragmatic tools for change. Its purpose is to create the possibility for there to be a world of consciousness and oneness.

What is consciousness you say? Consciousness includes everything and judges nothing. It includes every possibility that could exist. With absolutely no judgment of any of it—or of you. Does that sound like a world you'd like to live in? If so, read on! (If not, now's probably a good time to pass this book on to one of your weird friends or family members.)

Today I travel around the world, facilitating people with the tools of Access Consciousness. I've developed a unique way of working with groups of people, energies and bodies simultaneously, called *The Energetic Synthesis of Being (ESB)*.

Most of what I am sharing with you in this book, I've learned from exploring what else is possible together with the amazing participants in the ESB Classes. The places they are willing to go, and the other possibilities they are willing to explore totally blows me away—every time. People are far greater than they realize and more capable than they ever imagined.

During an ESB class, you are invited to access and be energies you never knew were available. And you'll do it together with the whole group. In the space of this class, you begin to synthesize with your being, your body and the Earth in a way that creates a more conscious life and a more conscious planet. By being these energies, by being you, you change everything: the planet, your life and everyone you come into contact with.

You are Being You, and you are Changing the World.

I've also been very fortunate to have the most phenomenal of facilitators, and co-creators, the founder of Access Consciousness, Gary Douglas, as my best friend. How did I get so lucky?

Please know this: these tools, perspectives and processes have changed lives for thousands of people all over the world! This is the reason I wrote this book. If you have ever said to yourself: *"There has to be something more than this!"*—this is my way of telling you: Yes! Yes. There is! There are people that are experiencing it right now!

This is *one* possible path to a completely different way of being in the world—leading your life consciously, and being the difference the Earth requires.

Will it work for you? Will this book guide you to BE YOU? And will that truly change the world?

Only you know, my friend. Only you can choose for you.
So, what do you know?

And is it possible this is the invitation you've been waiting for?
Is now the time?

I will do whatever it takes to show you the possibilities. Your job is just to stay out of judgment and conclusion long enough to see if these possibilities are something you would like to choose. Will you come along? Wanna play?

Are you ready? Let's go!

Weird

Do you know the original meaning of the word 'weird'?

Weird: Of spirit, fate and destiny

Does that sound like you?
Just a little bit?
Would you be willing to let go of the illusion that you are average, normal and real ... and just like everyone else?

Would you instead be willing to be as weird, wonderful and
AMAZING as you truly be?

Starting now?

Good Book!

Because this book is designed to create change, it will probably confuse or annoy you at times. If you don't understand something, or if it feels incomplete, many times the information needed for you to understand it will be presented a few short pages ahead of where you are in the book.

How does it get any better than that?

Please also know, many parts of this book are designed to get you to question what is true for you, rather than presenting you with a point of view that you are supposed to buy.

These parts may seem incomplete to you, but they were left that way on purpose, so you can come to your own knowing as you ponder. So if you find yourself questioning, or wondering—this little book is doing it's job.

Good book! Good book!

PART I

Being You....

"We spend our entire lives trying to prove that we are not what we never were in the first place."

—Mel C.

What if you started to embrace reality on your terms?
What if your reality was something ... completely different?
What if a completely different reality is exactly what is required?

Is now the time?

─────────── TOOL ───────────

Destroy, Uncreate, Set Your Reality Free

If you look at this book, it looks solid, right? Except science tells us its 99.999 percent space. But it does look solid. Isn't that weird? Yet, it is 99.999 percent space—it's just that the molecules are arranged in such a way that it looks solid and impenetrable.

What if the limitations in your life and in your body, every single one of them, were exactly the same way? What if they looked really solid, and that's the only way you've been able to see them until now?

I know it sounds strange ... and yet, what I will invite you to, if you are willing to receive it, is the awareness that those things are not necessarily solid, never were solid, and don't have to be solid anymore.

I'd like to invite you—and the energy you are—to go back to the place where you took all these molecules and arranged them as solid instead of space, pliability and changeability, and undo it so it can be the space that it actually is. So you can be the space you truly be.

That's all. And so much more than that!

In order to get there, sometimes in this book I will be asking you to give something up. Actually, I may ask you to destroy and uncreate it.

It may seem crazy at the time.

Why would I ever ask you to do this? Because whenever you're willing to destroy and uncreate and let go of something that is limiting you, it automatically and instantly opens up the space for something less limited or even unlimited to show up. Does that makes sense? Let go of the limited and the unlimited finally has space to exist.

Yet, please stop a second and ask yourself:
Am I willing to do this?

If you get a yes, what do you have to lose?

Everything you are willing to give up, uncreate, and
destroy, opens up a totally different possibility in
your life.

You can never give up what you Be. Your very Being is
undestructible.

You can only let go of, uncreate and destroy what is defining you limiting
you, and keeping you and your being stuck, which makes room for
something different and greater to show up.

If you like, I would highly suggest adding this clearing statement after:

*Right and Wrong, Good and Bad, POD and POC, All Nine, Shorts, Boys and
Beyonds* (POD and POC for short). That's what I do.*

This statement asks the consciousness of you to go back to the point of
creation (or point of destruction), before you even planted the seed to this
limitation, and invite the seed to dissolve.

The funny and weird thing is that it … just does.
It works. Like magic.
What if magic is what you truly be?

What if you could consider this clearing statement as your magic wand—a
way to change ANY part of your life that you would like to change?

Wands out, let's go!

**If you'd like more of an explanation, please read more about the
Clearing Statement in the back of the book.*

Ask a Question….
Don't Look for Answers

I can hear you thinking already.

The wheels are turning:
Think, think, think.
Tick, tock, tick, tock.
Right, wrong, right, wrong.

Can this REALLY work?

Haven't you had enough of that darn machine you call your mind, and it's incessant search for the RIGHT answer yet?

Let me give you the way out of the right answer
universe:
ASK A QUESTION.

It really is that simple.

Here's how it works: most of us are going down the road of our life and we've already got a point of view of where we're headed, and that's the darn direction we're going. That's it. Basta!

Because we've decided that's the direction we're going, it's as though we erect these walls around us, to the left and right that we can't see over, can't see around, and can't see through. Our only option is to head in the direction we concluded we were going.

Without asking a question, we are left to wander the halls of the labyrinth we have created as though it is our only set of choices in life.

If you ask a question, all of a sudden doors open up to the left and to the right and they've got light and space behind them, exposing different rooms and other doorways of possibility. You open them up, and it's like, "Wow! There are possibilities I didn't even know existed before."

The question is the key to opening other doorways of possibility. You'll never see those doors and you'll never even know they are there—let alone be able to open them—if you don't ask a question.

When in doubt, ask a question.

Here are some great questions you can ask to open up more possibilities in many situations in your life:

*1. How does it get any better than this? (Ask this when
   something "good" happens or when something "bad" happens.)*

2. What's right about this I'm not getting?

3. What would it take to change this?

4. What else is possible?

*5. What would it take for this to turn out better than I could have
   imagined?*

*6. Who am I today and what grand and glorious adventures am
   I going to have?*

And don't start looking for the answer, please!

Here's how it usually works in this reality.
We ask a question, and then we go into our mind,
*"Is that the right answer? Is this the right answer?
Is this the right answer?"*

It's like taking a little seed, planting it, watering it, and the next day coming and picking it up out of the ground to see if it's growing yet. And when it isn't you say, *"No! Stupid seed! No flower yet."* So you plant and water it again and grab it the next day, *"Have you grown yet?!?! Like hello ... !?!?"* Is that the seed's fault? No. You haven't given it time to sprout and to take root.

I have a different suggestion for you:
Literally, when you ask a question—SHUT UP.

Now when I say that, that may seem unkind to some of you, so I apologize.
And just shut up! Okay?

Ask a question and just go quiet for a moment … an hour … a day …
or a month … and let the energy pervade your universe.
Not a right answer—an energy.

That energy is the result of the question you just asked. Whenever you ask
a question, an energy "comes up." It presents itself. It makes itself known
to you. It's that energy that was your reason for asking the question in the
first place.

This is why you asked the question in the first place—to open the door to
getting the energy which would guide you to the thing for which you were
asking.

So let's ask a question:

*What gift can this book be to you that you couldn't even imagine when
you bought, borrowed, found, stole, or were gifted it?*

Now, my friend, shut up and read :)

Beyond This

Reality

What Is Energy?

Have you ever given someone a hug and just felt like you could stand there forever ... melting ... falling into the person you are hugging ... ? And, by contrast, have you ever given someone a hug where it felt like hugging a rock on legs?

Are those two experiences different? Then you know what I mean when I talk about energy. Those are two totally different energetic experiences—two totally different "energies."

It is that simple.

(On another level, it can also be infinitely complex—part of which we'll be exploring together in this book.)

Imagine yourself walking in a deep, deep forest. There are no roads, just trails made by elves and fairies. The sunbeams are tainted green by the roof of leaves.

You walk on this living Earth, and it is softness under your feet. There is a single woodpecker knocking softly at your heart while you breathe in the scent of summer....

Now close your eyes and stand still for a second, here in the forest.

How you be?

The forest has no judgments of you, and no reality to validate. It is one of the places where Being comes easy.

Now close your eyes again and walk down the main street of your home-town, or through the office where you work ... or up the stairs to your parents' home.

Is there a difference in how you be?

What is that? What would it be like if your town and everyone in it, would receive you with no judgment, as the forest does? Who—and how—could you *choose* to be then?

Everything that doesn't allow you to choose that right now, will you please destroy and uncreate that? Right and Wrong, Good and Bad, POD and POC, All Nine, Shorts, Boys and Beyonds.™

— Chapter 1 —
Your Reality and the Free-Will Universe

Before we go on, let's define REALITY....

What I mean by reality is basically the common, average, ordinary way everybody learns to function here on this planet—the things we all have in common—and the things we THINK are REAL, without really thinking about it. It's all the stuff that seems like it just IS to such a degree that we often don't ever question it.

In order to create a reality you have to have two people or more who align and agree on a point of view. In other words, a reality gets created any time two or more people conclude, "This is the way it is," even if they don't do it cognitively. That's actually how a reality gets created. Did you know that?

So when I say this reality, I'm actually talking about what you were handed when you were born—the rules and regulations of your family, the rules and regulations of your society, the rules and regulations of the planet, all the physical laws of reality—all that stuff.

For example, the rules of this reality say that you can't move your body from here to Fiji instantaneously. I say—why not? Let's change that! Wouldn't it be a lot more fun?

We may not succeed in changing it today, but let's head in that direction and see what shows up. As a motivational speaker in high school who changed my life with this phrase says, "Shoot for the moon! If we miss and hit the stars, that's not half-bad."

Instead we are trying to make all the parts of this reality work right so we can be happy—rather than creating what we would really like to have, even if it's totally different than this reality. We think there must be something right about this reality if everybody's choosing it and everybody's telling us it's right. I mean, it must be right, right?

The ongoing scenario in our heads is something like: "Judgment must be right. Family must be right. School must be right. Money must be right. I'm probably the only one who doesn't get it right and keeps feeling wrong." But what if all these things that are supposed to be "right" are wrong for you?!

What if there were a totally different way of looking at this?

Here is one possibility to consider:
The reality you've been given does not work. You don't have to choose it anymore if you don't want to. With that awareness, what would you truly like to choose as your life?

If you truly knew that this were a FREE-WILL UNIVERSE, what would you start choosing right away?

༄ ༄ ༄

What if You Were the Master of Your Universe?

You've heard the idea that we live in a free-will Universe? We are told that this is one of the laws of the universe, one of the ways this weird and wacky place functions.

My question is: If that is true—why do our lives look the way they do?

Why does the world?

If it's a free-will universe then why do we keep believing that we can't choose to change? Change our money situation? Or the way our body feels? Or the relationships we keep creating over and over and over with the same person, just in a different body?

And why do we keep choosing trauma and drama, poverty, unhappiness, separation, anger, hate and judgment? Why is it we seem to be unable—or unwilling—to change all of that?

We may be cute, but we definitely aren't that bright. My point of view is that we must be missing something about the idea that it's a free-will universe.

So what I would like to do is take this idea of a free-will universe and invite you to recognize it. In other words, let's use your power to choose and your power to change. Let's use them to change the past that has been limited and not worked for you and create a different present and a different future—where you **be you, and change the world.**

Doesn't that sound like fun? I thought so!

We all seem to have this idea, this point of view, of exactly what it is going to take to have what we desire in life. What if something totally different were required? It must be!

If you don't have the world you'd like to live in and the life you'd like to have, then what you thought it was going to take to get that ... must be incorrect.

Does that make sense?

As long as we stick to the point of view that change can only occur in the one way we decided it would (that isn't working), we will always look in the wrong direction for the source of change. All of us!

Would you be willing to let go of, destroy and uncreate—at least for the time it takes you to read this book—all projections, expectations, separations, decisions, conclusions, judgments, rejections and points of view that you have bought of what it would take to change your life (and the world)? Right and Wrong, Good and Bad, POD and POC, All Nine, Shorts, Boys and Beyonds.™

Thank you. What else can show up now? I mean, really, what do you have to lose?

∽ ∽ ∽

Finding the Free-Will Universe
(Or, at least, how I started to find mine....)

See, I used to have a lot of answers, or at least I pretended I did.

Ten years ago, I was starting my second chiropractic practice, and I even had some patients. I was making almost enough to pay my rent: Oh Joy! I had a girlfriend that everybody said was the perfect girl for me. I had everything that was supposed to make you happy here, except loads of money, but that wasn't that important to me. I had tried every single modality for inner peace I could find, but I was still dying inside.

So I told the Universe; "*You have six months or I'm killing myself. I've been here working for you, trying to bring awareness to people, trying to change their lives and their bodies, and trying to change things for the better on the planet, and nothing is coming back to me. I hate waking up in the morning! If that's the way it's got to be—fine. But I'm killing myself. Either things change or I am out of here.*"

I didn't just mean out of my relationship or Santa Barbara, I meant out of this life.

"*There has got to be someplace happier, some other body, some other life. I'll come back as a gypsy, or a pacific islander, where I get to hang out in the islands all day. Or maybe I'll come back as a Rockefeller and have buckets of money. There has to be something different. There has to be something better. Maybe some other planet ... ???*"

I was willing to end it, because I got to the point where what was, was not enough. I knew it, and it gave me this place of being able to not have as valuable what I had decided was valuable in the past.

Everything that I had decided was valuable, I had. And it wasn't valuable. Do you know what I mean? Have you ever been there, even briefly, to that place? If so, this book will probably make a lot of sense to you.

Literally a week after I made this demand, I saw an ad in the paper, a tiny little classified ad. It said, *"Access: All of life comes to me with ease and joy and glory,"* and it had this girl's phone number.

My reaction was; *"Pollyanna put an ad in the paper!"* I was furious. *"My life is pain, suffering and gory! What are you talking about? Ease, joy and glory. What is that?"* I literally throttled the paper and threw it away. Now, this paper comes out once a week in Santa Barbara, and the next week I saw the ad again: *"Access: All of life comes to me with ease and joy and glory."*

ARGHHHH!

But long before seeing this ad, I had realized that if you're in total resistance to something, there's probably something in it for you, you just don't know what it is yet. So, since I just wanted to kill the person who put the ad in the paper, I called her and made an appointment. . . .

Call it Divine Inspiration, call it insanity, call it grasping for a lifeboat just before the Titanic that was my life made its final shuddering plunge into the abyss ... That phone call literally gave me access to my life, and I have not been able to squeeze myself into the box that used to be me ever again. I am so, so grateful.

I had a session with the girl, an Access Bars session, a simple process of touching points on the person's head. After this session I had the first sense of peace I'd had in almost three years. It was the first time I remember knowing everything was OK, everything always had been, and everything always would be ... and I never contemplated suicide again.

One tool, one thing, a process that took about an hour ... from someone I'd never even met before ... and it changed the energy of my whole life and what I knew was possible.

That is what I'm hoping to share with you in this book—the energetic awareness that a different energy is possible for you, too.

Because it's the energy of your life you're looking to change.

I used to do all these things, all these spiritual modalities, and think, *"I want to change this thing, and this thing...."* But even if the thing changed, if the energy was still the same, it didn't matter.

Do you know what I mean?

☙ ☙ ☙

The Vibration of You

When you change the energy, the outward situations of your life change, as if by magic. For example, have you ever noticed that people seem to move slower when you're in a huge hurry? Have you noticed that when you decide, for whatever reason, you're no longer in a hurry, that people speed up again? That's because you changed your energy.

Have you ever walked into a room and changed the energy of it without even trying? Or had a friend who was having a bad day and when you talked to them, or hugged them, they brightened up? What created that change? Was it what you said, or some psychological technique—**or your very being?**

It was your being that changed them. It is the energy you be ... the vibration of You ... the essence of you that is actually the totality of you that is the thing that exists beyond everything you think. It is you, embracing the entire world.

One of the things I have discovered is true is that when you step into being something, you simply become that energy. It invites everyone around you to be it, too—if they are willing to have it.

If they are not willing to have it, it puts that energy into their world so they can have it when they are ready. When they are ready. It could be twenty years from now. It could be a billion years from now. Who cares?

You're just stepping into *being* something. Having a new awareness of something and then choosing it allows *everyone else* on the planet to have it because you are willing to be it.

When you step into being something different you open up the space for that to exist where before there was no space for it to be.

I would like to invite you to the awareness of the energetic vibrations of being, the being that you be that you have never been willing to see before.

The energy you be.

The vibration you be.

And, it's probably something totally different than what you've ever thought it could be. Completely different.

But it is something that when you allow it to just be, the ease you've always wanted in your life can show up. The joy can show up, and the possibilities can show up—not from effort or thinking, but just because you're being you with such a presence that it can't be destroyed. From that place, which really isn't a place as you know it, you create things. You change things.

Would you be willing to find out who you truly be? Would you be willing to make the demand that you show up? Would you be willing to become acquainted with what's really true for you as a being?

Just ask. Right now.

In so doing, you'll open the door to a different world of possibility.

You don't have to figure out how!

It is the Universe's job to show you how that is going to happen.

All you do is make the demand! Then you just follow your life and your living and go where the Universe leads you. Pretty easy, right? More on the "how" later....

Oh, one more thing ... I KNOW YOU CAN DO IT!

Finding the Energy of Me

I got this amazing gift 10 years ago when Gary Douglas, the founder of Access Consciousness, walked into my office and asked for a session. I was practicing a chiropractic technique that had three "levels of care" at the time, and I had just started with Access Classes.

When he walked in, Gary said, "*Look, I know there are three levels of care to what you do. The first two levels don't work very well for me. I'm sorry. You are going to have to go straight to the third level.*"

Basically in my head I was saying, "*Oh crap. I have no idea what to do with this guy.*" I only had clients at Level 1 and Level 2 in my clinic at this time, and I had no idea how to treat someone in Level 3.

I just sat there until he said, "*Look, just ask my body what it wants. Follow the energy—you'll know what to do.*"

One part of me went into conclusion, thinking, "*What? I'll know what to do? Do you know who I am? I am the most pathetic practitioner of anything on the planet! I'm the biggest idiot you have ever met! I'm the one with an office about the size of a closet. I don't know anything.*" Another part went into question, "*I do?*"

When I started to work on him, I was in a completely different space. *I knew what to do.* Not cognitively, not in any way I could describe at the time. But my being knew. There was a knowing in me.

In that moment, I stepped into a space of being I didn't know existed previously. I stepped into being me. In that space, I had access to me and to my knowing. There was no thought—just knowing.

At one point while working on him, I was standing about 15 feet away from him, on the other side of the room, and he was flopping around on the table like a fish. I was moving my hand in the air, just because it "felt" like the right thing to do. Each time I would move my hand right, his head would turn right. Each time I moved my hand left, his head would turn left. He was face down! He couldn't see me at all.

That first session I had with him was the very first session I had ever done of something I now call the Energetic Synthesis of Being (ESB). It was the beginning of an entirely different way of working with bodies using the energy of the body and the being to erase limitation—permanently in many cases.

Now, I travel the world facilitating people with this ESB work. One of the greatest gifts I get is to receive the testimonials and the letters of gratitude from people whose lives are changed from it.

Please know, WE ALL have a capacity to create the world as a better place for ourselves and others—simply by being willing to BE US and be as different as we are. We just have to find out what this is for us and be willing to choose it. The world needs you. What are you waiting for?!

What do you know you've been pretending not to know or denying that you know about who and what you truly are? I didn't know what I knew until I became it. What can you become, if you just allow yourself to "let go and trust and be it?"

❧ ❧ ❧

Finding the Energy of You

If no one ever teaches you how to be, how can you step into an awareness of what it's like to be you?

One thing that can assist is to look for times in the past when you chose to truly be you. These were times when you had no thought, no judgment, total peace, and a joy in just being, with no point of view. Oh yeah, you probably also had a sense of exuberance and possibility. Those were the times when you were being you.

Let me give you an example from my life that may assist:

One year, I volunteered to ride in the California AIDS Ride. It's a 600-mile bike ride over the course of a week, and you ride from San Francisco to Los Angeles.

The reason I volunteered to be a rider for this amazing event is because the previous year, in my last year in chiropractic college, I volunteered as a student chiropractor to treat riders for the same event. All the money raised by the riders went to services for people who had HIV or AIDS. We were the ones helping the riders make it through the week. As chiropractic volunteers, we were on the front lines, treating the riders who desperately needed our services.

Many times over the course of the week-long event, I was brought to tears by the courage of the riders I had the fortune of treating. There were grandmothers, grandfathers, brothers, sisters, lovers, parents and friends, riding because their loved ones had HIV or were dying of AIDS.

There were people with HIV, who were riding to tell the disease: "You don't own me! You may eventually kill me, but not today, and not without a fight!" The courage these people had, and their lack of judgment, and the sense of communion we all shared inspire me to this day.

This ride was the one place I had been where there was a large group of people, and no one was judging anyone else. It was one of the first times I had ever experienced that everybody was there to assist and empower everyone else. There was a greatness that I perceived possible in that, and I said to myself: *"You know what, I've got to contribute to this. Next year I'm going to ride this damn thing!"*

Even though I hadn't been on a bike since I was 16, I made the demand that I get a bike and learn to ride it. I bought a bike from a fellow chiropractic student that was a former racer. I started out very slowly at first, and trained myself for several months. I did everything I could to raise the $2,500 required to ride, and I had some amazingly generous people donate to me so that I could pursue this dream.

Finally, after months of preparation and fund-raising and learning to actually ride a bike again, I was on the ride! I was riding alongside people who should not have been able to ride a bike 600 miles ever—and they were there riding because it meant so much to them. As it did the previous year, the ride opened my being to a whole new awareness of what we, as people working together, are capable of.

On the really long hills, many people were like, *"I don't think I can make this, I think I'm going to die first."* On many of them, I would ride up the hill and then I would ride back down, cheering people on from the other side of the road, and then I would ride back up the same hill again, still cheering and yelling, "Riders, you can do it! This hill can't stop you! You're kicking its butt! Go riders!"

This was one of the first times in my adult life that it was clear to me beyond a shadow of a doubt that I was being a contribution to other people. When these people saw that someone cared about them enough to cheer them on, (and ride these amazingly long hills twice to do so), it gave many of them the strength to continue.

One lady, apparently remembering my registration number and my bike, came up to me at a rest stop and told me that my riding back down the hill and cheering the riders on inspired her to continue riding that day. She said she was almost exhausted, and she asked God for help, and 20 minutes later I rode by, cheering like a crazy man. She said she laughed and cried and carried on. At which point I cried, we embraced, and I realized what a gift we can all be to each other if we choose to be it.

In that gifting I was also receiving so much contribution, simultaneously, it's hard to put into words. So I hope you get the energy I'm trying to convey. This is one of the examples that I've got from my life of what it feels like when I'm truly being me, with no judgment, no point of view, but also with a sense of exuberance and possibility.

When I rode in this event, riding up and down the hills a second time, *I could no longer deny the energy of what it was like to be me. How much energy have you used against you to deny the energy of what it's like to truly be you? Everything that is, will you destroy and uncreate all that, please and claim and acknowledge how amazing you really are? Right and Wrong, Good and Bad, POD and POC, All Nine, Shorts, Boys and Beyonds.™ Thank you.*

That week changed my whole life, and I've been different ever since. It is part of the reason I had the courage to stay alive when I really wanted to kill myself. Somewhere, I knew that energy and possibility for being was there, because I could never totally deny it after the experience I had on the AIDS Ride. I knew it was there. I just couldn't access it at the time.

Why this story from my life? To get you to look at yours. When have you been so dynamically, unquestionably you, with the exuberance, the peace, and the no-judgment you know you really are?

Not everyone can go on an AIDS Ride, so let me give you a slightly different example. When I was six years old, my Mom took me to Idaho to visit my grandparents, aunts, uncles, and other family members. One of the great things about those years in a small town in Idaho was that a six-year-old could walk to the local store on his own.

That is just what I did! I went to the store, and I took all the money that I received from my latest birthday (that I had been saving up for my trip), and I used it all to buy little tins of lip gloss for my grandmother and each aunt and uncle that I was going to visit.

It brought me such joy to hand them each my little gift! It apparently brought them joy, too. They smiled and most of them cried, especially when, unbeknownst to me, my mother let them know that I had taken all of my own money, gone to the store on my own, and purchased these items because I wanted to give them a gift.

This is another example that I have looked back on when I have wanted to know what it feels like to be me. I think of the generosity that six-year-old had, and that willingness to spend his last penny to make others happy. I think of that whenever I feel strange about money or whenever I feel in judgment of me. Somehow, it reminds me that there's something else available for me to choose.

The really important question here ... what else is available for you to choose ... that you haven't chosen ... maybe for a very long time???

Everything that doesn't allow you to be everything you truly can be, will you please destroy and uncreate it all now? Right and Wrong, Good and Bad, POD and POC, All Nine, Shorts, Boys and Beyonds.™ Thank you.

Having your reality is not about anyone else, nor does it require anyone else's point of view, nor is it dependent on anyone else for you to have it. You can have it now! (If you'll demand it.)

Would you be willing to demand that more of your life show up like that now? And everything that doesn't allow that to show up for you, will you destroy and uncreate all that now, please? Right and Wrong, Good and Bad, POD and POC, All Nine, Shorts, Boys and Beyonds.™ Thank you.

Would you please now look over your life at three times when you KNOW you were truly being you, and write them below, with some details to jog your memory and awareness? These were times when you had no judgment, total peace, a joy in being alive, and probably a sense of exuberance, too. Hopefully, the examples I've given you will assist. Don't think too much about it. Just go with the first three examples that come to mind. And if you have more than three, please keep writing. Please use another piece of paper if you require one.

1. _____

_____

_____

_____

2. _____

_____

_____

_____

3. _____

_____

_____

_____

If you use these three examples you just wrote down, you'll have an awareness of what it's like to truly be you, so that you have something to aim for,
something to recall as the energy of you, and something to request of the
Universe to gift you more of. These examples are what it feels like when
you are truly being you. That feeling, that energy, is your new starting point.

For the next 3 days, every time you think about it, just recall one of these
times when you were truly being you and ask this question, "What will it
take for more of that to show up now?"

You are on your way to having more of you already! How does it get any
better than that?

✎ ✎ ✎

Getting the Living You Truly Desire:
You, the Universe, and the Energy Bubble

Most of us have been told that in order to create something, we need to put
our desire "out there" in order to create it. I have found that it is just the
opposite. I've found that inviting in what you'd like your life to be is far more
effective. Wanna give it a shot? (Please know, this IS NOT visualization.
It's creation by request of the Universe. It's a way of asking and receiving
from the infinitely gifting Universe we live in by speaking its language—that
of energy.)

Ready for something different???

So here it goes: Call up the energy of what you'd truly like to have as your life. "If you could ask for and have anything at all, what would it be? If there were ABSOLUTELY NO LIMITATIONS in your world regarding time, money, creative and generative capacity, what would you ask for?

If you had a magic wand that could make anything come true for you now, what would you choose right away? Now, get the way it would FEEL to have all of those things showing up for you.

Don't think too much about it, just ask for it—whatever it is.

Would you like to be able to have a nice home that has a particular feel to it? I'm not saying get the picture of a four bedroom, three bathroom place … *No, get the way it would feel to you to have the place in which you'd love to live.*

Would you like to be able to travel? Would you like to do work you thoroughly enjoyed? Every day when you went to do whatever it is you do, it was exciting, joyful, new and it changed all the time and gave you more of you every single day? Would that be exciting for you? Get the way that would feel, too.

I'm just giving you some possibilities, you can add any of your own that you desire.

So get the way that would feel, put that energy in front of you, sort of like an energy bubble if you will. Now what kind of relationships and/or sex would you like to have there? If you could have anything in that realm, what would it feel like to have that—to wake up with that, to have that in your life, to have it around you, with you?

What kind of relationships would you have with your family, your friends, what kind of relationship would you have with the planet and with the plants? With the animals? With the oceans? With the earth itself and the very land under our feet? What type of fun would you like to allow yourself to have and be? Get the way that would feel.

How would you feel on a daily basis if you could have it? Put that in there, too.

Now pull energy into that "energy bubble" of feeling from all over the Universe.

Keep pulling. ∽ ∽ ∽ ∽ *More.* ∽ ∽ ∽ ∽ *More.* ∽ ∽ ∽ ∽

More. ∽ ∽ ∽ ∽ *And even more….*

The Universe is very large and it desires to gift to you, so … pull MORE!

There. That's it!

What should be happening is that your heart is opening up, as you pull more energy into these things you actually desire. It's a really big universe, don't stop where you are. BIG universe. Thank you.

Pull energy into it from all over the Universe, keep pulling, keep pulling, and keep pulling until your heart really opens up.

When it does … be with the energy of it for a moment … and then … let little trickles go out to everyone and everything that's going to help make that a reality for you from all over the Universe that you don't even know yet.

This "energy bubble" you created based on getting how it would "feel" to have your life show up the way you desire it is not actually based on just feelings. It's based on an awareness of the energy that would be there if you actually had what you are asking for. It's just that "feeling" is the easiest way to describe it.

So, go for that "feeling" because you'll be going for the energy of the living you'd like to create. After all, you chose it. Let's create it! *Everything that doesn't allow that to show up, will you destroy and uncreate it please? Right and Wrong, Good and Bad, POD and POC, All Nine, Shorts, Boys and Beyonds.*™

All of the projections, expectations, separations, judgments, and rejections you have about what life has to be that don't allow your living to be what it could be, will you destroy and uncreate that please? Right and Wrong, Good and Bad, POD and POC, All Nine, Shorts, Boys and Beyonds.™

That's a way of having an energy that you can follow to generate the living you desire. When something shows up and has that energy to it (in other words, when it feels the way that "energy bubble" feels), you can choose to go there.

For example, if you're deciding between two different jobs, and one feels a lot more like that energy, do that one. Or if you're deciding between two different people to date and one feels a lot more like that energy bubble, date that one. And so on ... with food, cars, trips, houses, courses to attend, books to buy, etc. In that way, you'll know whether a person, a class, or a book will contribute to the life you'd really like to have before you ever spend any time or money on it! How does it get any better than that?

Now you may get closer to this energy of your living, you may get further away from it—but it can ALWAYS be an awareness of what it's like to choose for you.

You can use that as a litmus test for something you're going to choose:

Does this feel like that energy bubble? Is this going to get me closer to what I desire? Does this give me more of me? Does this get me closer to having more of me, or does it get me further away?

Then at least you'll know—you know!—and it can be a guideline for every single choice you make from here on out.

The energy of you, the energy of your living.

--- **TOOL** ---

Light = True. You Just KNOW.

Try out the energy of the words in this book.
How do they land in you? Lightly or heavily?

Now, please know that what's true always makes you feel lighter. A lie always makes you feel heavier.

If it makes you feel lighter, it is true for you—however strange the words may sound. Maybe not true for anyone else. Still, true for you.

Let me say that again:

Something that's true for you always makes you feel lighter. A lie always makes you feel heavier.

Yes, I've said that twice now. But twice might not be nearly enough for you to believe me. You see, one of the rules of this reality is that you're not supposed to
be able to just know.

Yet, it's one of your most basic capacities.

This is a way of knowing everything that is right—for you—and everything that is "wrong"—for YOU. But because we're taught that we can't just KNOW, we spend our entire lives trying to figure everything out.

What if you just KNOW? What if it's much *simpler—and much quicker*—than trying to figure anything out? Which is quicker, thinking or knowing? Knowing, right?

What if what's true for you just makes you feel light? What's not—doesn't. Haven't you wanted an easy way to have an awareness of what's true for you, your whole life? Wouldn't that make your life A LOT easier? Well then, here it is again:

The truth always makes you feel lighter. A lie always makes you feel heavier.

So even if what you read here goes contrary to everything you thought before you opened this book—if it makes you feel lighter it's probably true for you.

If it makes you feel heavier then it's a lie. So, if you read something in this book that makes you feel heavier, it's either not true for you personally, or it conflicts with something you decided was true in the past. If it's really not true for you, DON'T BUY IT! You can still receive all the other parts of this book that are true for you.

Now the weird part is this: some of the greatest limitations we create are the things we've decided are true … that actually are not.

Say you decide that your mother truly hates you. Or let's say you decide that there is a lack of caring or love in the world. Try those out. Do they make you feel lighter? If so, it is true. If it makes you feel heavier, it is a lie.

Please know this: Buying a point of view from someone else, even if it's true for them, will always make you feel heavier, too, because it isn't true for you. It isn't your point of view, sweet dear beautiful you.

What is true for you will always make you feel lighter. Always. If it's heavy, it's a lie, or it's not your point of view. Period. Really. Honest.

In this book we're going to look at many of the things you may have bought as true for you even when they weren't and even though they may not serve you anymore. Would you be willing to choose something completely different now? How? Here's the beginning:

Please use this tool while reading this book! Again, and again, and again—ask the question, *light or heavy?*

Even if you don't think you know what that is or how it feels. As you ask this question (which is really applying a very simple but dynamic tool) you will get the awareness of what this light and heavy thing is all about.

As one woman in a class I was giving put it: *"I was asking if things were light or heavy—thinking I wasn't getting anything. Then 1 day, 3 weeks later, I just KNEW. I asked a question, and I KNEW! And rather than leave me, that knowing has continued to grow. Sure, I deny it sometimes (mostly when I want to make a choice that I know won't work out well for me), but this one tool has changed EVERYTHING for me. Thank you!"*—L.H., Denver, Colorado, USA.

Here's another way to use this tool: If something is light for you when you hear it or think of doing it, then that's usually the result that will get created in your life if you choose that thing. If it feels heavy when you think about doing it, that's usually the result that will get created.

So, for example, let's say you're at your local coffee shop, having your triple-caff-extra-fat-quadruple-sugar-caramel coffee concoction with double whipped cream and you start a conversation with a really attractive man. Though he appears to scoff at your coffee selection, while ordering his non-fat, decaf, herbal tea with no sugar, he asks you out. Though you don't know why, you get a weird heaviness as soon as he pops the question. That heaviness is an indication of what will happen if you accept his offer of a date. Why? Because as soon as you get asked out, you can see the future that will occur if you say yes or no. YOU KNOW—and that's how this works.

You know, though you don't desire to know that you know these things. But if you look back over your life, haven't you always known? Haven't you always been aware of when something wasn't going to turn out well for you? In this example, you don't even have to go on the date to get the information about how it will turn out. Something that feels lighter will turn out lighter—for you.

In the case of the date above, it could be that the attractive man was actually not only attractive but judgmental of one's food choices—or maybe just judgmental in general.

In case you haven't figured it out yet, judgmental people are not fun to hang out with. It's always heavy when you are being judged—for anything. (Here's a nice thing to know: unless they are family, you can choose not to hang out with judgmental people if you don't want to.)

One more thing: If you want to have an enjoyable life, make choices that make you feel light when you think about them, because those are the ones that will lead to more lightness when you choose them.

Beyond

— Judgment —

The Kings and Queens of Judgment

Why is it that the most limited person always wins on this planet?

Why do we always give up our reality and awareness and back down from the person with the most limited point of view and the most judgment?

Why is it that you say, "*Oh, they must be right because they are judging me so harshly?*" Or, "*Oh, they must be right because they are so mean.*"

That they judge you so harshly does not mean they are right, my beautiful friend.

It just means that they are the king or queen of judgment.

— Chapter 2 —
I Am.
Therefore I Am Wrong.
Right?

Do you have somebody in your life that doesn't judge you at all? Even one person?

If you have one person that doesn't judge you, do you notice how healing and nurturing it is to be around them? How after just 10 minutes in their company your whole being and your body relax?

What if you were that person?

For you?

How would you be perceived if someone were willing to perceive all of you with no judgment? How would you perceive you, if you perceived all of you with no judgment?

Haven't you wanted that your whole life?

However, you always place a criterion on it. You say; *"I can have that if …
I am perfect."* Or, *"I can have that if … it matches with what everyone else in my life
knows is possible."* Or, *"I can have that if … I can finally get rid of everything I decided
is wrong with me."* Or, *"I can have that if … I can finally make my parents (or my
significant other) happy."*

What if you instead say, *"OK, I will choose and demand that I stop judging me and
step into what it would be like to perceive, know, be and receive all of me without judgment,
perfect or not."*

*Everything that doesn't allow that to show up, times a godzillion, will you destroy and
uncreate all that please? Right and Wrong, Good and Bad, POD and POC, All Nine,
Shorts, Boys and Beyonds.™ Thank you.*

What if that were the possibility? Would you consider having more of
that? Even though nobody ever taught you how? For me, that's an essential
aspect of being you—perceiving, knowing, being and receiving you without
judgment. One of the greatest sadnesses in this world to me is that no one
ever teaches us that this is valuable, let alone how to be it.

People teach you how to fit into this reality. They teach you how to judge.
They teach you how to separate from others, and make yourself wrong,
how to try to win, and how not to lose, and supposedly how to get it right
here. But they never teach you how to Be. They teach you how to think,
how to take tests, how to drive, how to read, how to do math. But they never
teach you how to Be.

When I talk about this idea of being, it isn't something you learn. But, it is
something you can choose to Be. Often that takes a lot of UN-learning on
our part. What if Be-ing looked completely different than you thought?

What if There Were Nothing Wrong with You?

Have you ever noticed how it is healing and nurturing to be around little kids? You know why? Because you are not being judged. They see you as a being with no point of view. You actually allow yourself to be you with no judgment.

Children don't have a point of view that you should be any different than you are right now. You are not a wrongness in their eyes. How much of your life have you spent believing you are a wrongness?
OK, this is something I know:
There is nothing wrong with you.
You are not a wrongness.
You are one of the greatest rightnesses the Universe has ever seen.

We've been taught to create our entire lives through judgment, except those rare moments of space we have in our lives. 99.999999999999 percent of your life, you are functioning from judgment.

Now, the cool thing is that even when you read the above sentence, you go:

"Oh my God! I'm so bad! I'm so wrong for doing that!"

That, my beautiful friend, is judgment. Of you. Again.

If there were nothing wrong with you and nothing to undo—where would you start? Where would you begin? What would you choose?

Most of us are trying to undo the wrongness before we even start. We know there must be some major inherent wrongness in us, because we can feel it in our bones. Really that is all we are sure about.

Then you think, *"If I just get the right relationship, or enough money, or the cutest kids on the planet, then it will all stop feeling wrong."* But then you get all those things, and it still feels wrong. You know why? Because the idea that there is anything wrong with you is a lie, and you can't change a lie into a truth. You can only acknowledge it's a lie and stop buying it!

So, let's look at what's valuable in this reality for a moment … One of the big things that is really valuable in this reality is judgment—as though that's awareness, as though that's a way of creating something.

But every time you judge, you separate from the person or thing you're judging; but in order to do that, don't you also have to separate from you? *Everything you've created and instituted to separate from you by buying the lie that judgment is real and true for you, will you please destroy and uncreate all that please? Right and Wrong, Good and Bad, POD and POC, All Nine, Shorts, Boys and Beyonds.*™ *Thank you.*

✍ ✍ ✍

Does Your Life Have Anything to Do with You?

I once met this man at a class I was giving in Montreal. Ten years earlier, he had gotten to the point where he sold his company and made more money than anybody could hope to make. He was "set for life." He had the cars, he had the houses, he had the women, and he got the paycheck—and all he could think was, *"Is this it?"*

This reality tells you if you have enough money, if you have this kind of car, this kind of house, this kind of relationship, then you'll be happy, and you'll feel fulfilled. *Ask yourself: is that true for me?*

No matter in what area you have this reality as the standard for a successful life, when you achieve it, it's still never enough. Why? *Because it doesn't include you.*

People I work with tell me: *"I have been doing this relationship, but it has nothing to do with me."* I ask, *"How much of the rest of your life has anything to do with you?"* And they realize, *"Oh my God. None of it."*

Most people living their normal, average, ordinary lives don't get that. Of course, it goes against everything we have learned about validating other people's points of view and defending this reality at all costs.

I look around, and I see most people proving that what they are choosing is right and proving the rightness that they've decided that they must have, while feeling in their own universe that they are somehow wrong. Put simply, they are trying desperately to get everything "right" while feeling that they must somehow be terribly wrong. This point of view ends up running their lives. They don't even know why they are wrong. They just know *that* they are wrong.

Whatever the reason and justification is, it keeps them from ever seeing themselves. It keeps them from ever having what it is they'd truly like to generate and create in life. It keeps them from ever being truly at peace or truly happy. Has this been the case for you too? *It doesn't have to be this way.*

A large part of the reason I was contemplating killing myself 11 years ago was because I was so tired of the unceasing feeling pervading my life that there was something wrong with me that I couldn't change. I—and the thousands of people I've worked with in the last 11 years—are living proof that it doesn't have to be this way. This can change! It's why I wrote this book—so that you'll know that the level of change you've been asking for does exist.

So, if you've been feeling wrong, or if you've been believing that you can't change what you desperately desire to change, just acknowledge that's where you are right now. That willingness to have that vulnerability with yourself can change your whole life.

Then ask:

What else is possible?

(Did you notice that, too, is a question?)

Mr. DeMille, I'm Ready for My Close-Up!

How many times in your life do you feel like you are just playing a role? *"Why am I playing this role? I don't even want to play this role? Where is my choice here?"* At some point in your life you decided what role you would play, and then you picked the character, the costume and the contribution to that role in all different situations. Why? Just because you did.

On the one hand, it sort of feels like you're living somebody else's life or somebody else's point of view, yet you keep going back to playing that role as though that's the sum total of you and the only choice you have.

There are some women who pick the role of being the starring lady. They are the starring lady wherever they are and whatever they do. They walk into the room and everybody goes, *"Oh, there is the starring lady."*

How did that happen? How did we all know? Because that is the role they chose.

Even if the character they portray is different in every moment and situation, they are still the starring lady. Your role could be, "I am the most emotional one," or "I am the richest one," or "I am the sex star," or "I am the poor victim." Or it could be something completely different. Only you know.

As an example, some people decide: *"My role is to be the garbage collector and a pile of debris. So, how am I going to do that with my family? Oh yeah, I'll pick a family where everyone else is rich, and I have no way of making money so I can feel like a pile of debris all the time. How am I going to do that in relationship? I'll choose someone who doesn't like me and tells me so all the time! How will I do that at work? I know! I will go and work at McDonalds© and never leave."*

Doing their roles—most people seem to be talking from their own library of tapes.

This is tape number 27:

"How are you today? I went to see a wonderful movie. It was amazing. What do you think about Barack Obama? Could change really occur? I don't think so. What about John McCain? I don't know about him either. He's perhaps a politician, too. Republican from what I hear."

You've got the Stepford wives, Stepford children, Stepford men. They are tape number 27, tape number 432, tape number 37. Oh, you responded with tape number 30, tape number 31. Tape number 31a. You responded with tape number 36, I'll respond with tape number 36a.

That's how most people communicate. Most people are not present. All they're doing is this tape, and the next tape, and the next. It's like they are in a whirlwind of nothingness talking.

Does that truly work for you?

Or, when tape number 31 starts yet again, does it feel like your entire life has been a lie?

I believe most of us feel that way somewhere. Some of us feel it about our entire lives. Some of us feel it only about 90% of our lives. People who are really happy feel it only about 85% of their lives.

But how many of us look and say, *"You know what, I feel like my life has nothing to do with me."* Instead you keep saying, *"No, I've got to get it right. I've got to get it right. Let me just control this. I've got to get it right. Let me control this. I've got to get it right. Let me control this. I just need this one thing to change, and then I'll really have it right ..."* Rather than looking at it and saying, *"You know what? I feel like I've got it so f***ing wrong, I don't want anyone to know how wrong I've got it—including me."*

See, this is the thing you've got to get: It often feels more real to you to take yourself out of the computation of your life, than it does to have you present in it.

What if you were so present and aware of what you desired as your life that nobody could pull you away from it, because you wouldn't be validating anyone's reality, but would instead be totally aware of yours—and unswaying in your demand to create it?

Everything that doesn't allow that to occur for you now, will you please destroy and uncreate all that please? Right and Wrong, Good and Bad, POD and POC, All Nine, Shorts, Boys and Beyonds.™

That would be weird, eh?

Would you be willing to have some more of that? What if everything that didn't work in your life were simply because you chose and have been playing these roles that didn't work for you?

๛ ๛ ๛

What if You Could CHOOSE Which Role to Play?

Would you be willing to try something different? I am not saying to throw away your roles, your characters and costumes. I am saying to be aware of them, and be aware of when you choose them. What if instead of believing that you are your role, you could choose your roles—and generate a life that actually feels real and true to you?

It's perfectly OK to play a role when necessary. It would be insane to expect that you could just give up all of them. Why would you? You have roles that you have to play because the people in your life expect certain things of you.

Just know when you're playing a role—choose to play the role when necessary. In this way, you own the role, and can use it to make your life better, rather than having it own you and running your life on autopilot.

Here are some questions you can use to give yourself different choices and possibilities the next time you have a choice to make:

1. Am I playing a role in this situation? If I were truly being me in this situation, what would I choose? *Everything that doesn't allow that to show up, will you destroy and uncreate all that now please? Right and Wrong, Good and Bad, POD and POC, All Nine, Shorts, Boys and Beyonds.*™

2. If I were not choosing this role right now, what could I choose instead? *Everything that doesn't allow that to show up, will you let all that go now please? Right and Wrong, Good and Bad, POD and POC, All Nine, Shorts, Boys and Beyonds.*™

3. If I had options that were greater than what I've ever considered in the past, what would I choose? *Everything that doesn't allow that to show up, will you let all that go now please? Right and Wrong, Good and Bad, POD and POC, All Nine, Shorts, Boys and Beyonds.*™

4. If I could choose anything I wanted here, what would I choose? *Everything that doesn't allow that to show up, will you let all that go now please? Right and Wrong, Good and Bad, POD and POC, All Nine, Shorts, Boys and Beyonds.*™

5. If I had a magic wand, and could have this turn out any way I wanted, how would it show up? Then USE YOUR MAGIC WAND! POC AND POD everything that doesn't allow it to show up that way. *Right and Wrong, Good and Bad, POD and POC, All Nine, Shorts, Boys and Beyonds.*™

∽∽∽∽

For All Those of You That Don't Feel Like You're from This Planet

Here comes something a bit strange. You can skip it if you like. Just please check if it feels light to you first....

See, there appears to be two different types of people, almost like two different species on the planet. We affectionately call them different names, but lets start with cow people and horse people, okay?

Cow people, they are the ones that know they are right. You know how cows are willing to just stay in the field and chew their cud and wait to be turned into hamburger and that's okay with them? They don't ever really want to move very fast. They don't want to change anything, and they'd be much happier just sitting in one spot, not really moving, not really doing too much … and never changing anything.…

Now the thing about cow people is that they always know they're right. They're always right, and you're always wrong. They don't question. They don't need to, because they know they're right.

They're consuming the planet at a very rapid rate, not questioning anything, and wanting to get theirs before the planet is eaten up, before anybody else gets theirs.

What a cow person would say is:

"You know what, you really need to stop doing all that weird sh*t you're doing! Why do you keep searching and doing weird stuff? Can't you get over that? Can't you finally be happy just sitting on the couch like a couch potato, flipping channels and drinking beer? Oh, by the way, global warming isn't real." That's a cow person's point of view.

The other kind of people—horse people—on the other hand, always ask: *"What else is possible?"*
You know how horses like to run and jump and play and have sex and eat and run and jump and have sex and run and jump and play and have sex and eat and then:
"What else can I do? I wonder if I can jump over that? Oh my, I did that! Did you see? Come on, check it out and jump over that! That was so much fun! Where else can we jump? Where else could we go? What else is possible?"

That's a horse person's point of view.
If you're one of those people who has spent your entire life looking for something different, you're a horse person.

I would call you a humanoid.

Horse people: humanoids. Cow people: humans.

It doesn't matter which you are.

My guess would be that since you haven't thrown this book out of the window yet, you are probably a humanoid.

Please know this: I may still irritate you immensely.

Immensely!

✑ ✑ ✑

Are You Willing to Be as Different as You Truly Be?

Most humanoids have been in judgment of themselves their entire lives wondering why they can't fit in, why they're not happy doing the same job for 20 years punching widgets, getting a plastic watch, retiring and dying. If you've ever wondered, *"Why doesn't that work for me, when it works for everyone else?"* then you're a humanoid.

What you have to get is that humans do not desire to change. They won't ever desire to change until humanoids (you) get that being different is actually valuable.

Then humans will choose a different possibility because they want to be like everybody else. That is their point of view. Right now everybody else is judgmental, mean, unkind, separating from everybody and trying to consume everything. That's the majority on the planet.

So guess what—until you step into being the difference that you are— the non-judgment, the kindness, the caring, the joy, the peace, the connection, and the awareness of a different possibility, humans won't have any motivation to do so.

I'm not saying that humanoids are better, or humans are bad or inferior, what I'm saying is that they're different. **You are different!**

How often do you feel like you don't belong?

Why do you think that is? It's because you're a different type of person—maybe even a different species. You don't fit in with any status quo, ever, and if you do, you resist and react like crazy because you actually hate fitting in—while acting like you desire it.

Am I right?

Stop!

Some of you started to feel uneasy. Some of you are thinking: "He is judging humans. *He is judging all those people I grew up with who still live in the same city, on the same street, and who have had the same job since they got out of high school.*"

That's the one thing you won't do: judge someone else ... Of course, you're perfectly happy judging yourself. You're perfectly willing to allow those same people you wouldn't judge to judge you. You do that nonstop, all day in and all day out. But you would never want to judge anybody else ... because that wouldn't be nice.

What if this whole conversation wasn't about judging humans? What if it were about getting you out of judgment of you for being different? What if it's about acknowledging a difference in how people <u>choose</u> to function? That's all it is.

What if you could just acknowledge: *"It's OK to be me. I'm just different. Now what?"*

Let's Test It: Are You Really Judgmental?

How many times over the course of your life, or even while reading this book have you had this little sneaking thought that you might actually be VERY judgmental? A big, bad judgmental person.

Let me tell you something (and please etch this one into your brain):
If you've EVER had the thought that you are judgmental—you are NOT.

Somebody who's judgmental doesn't ever think that they are judgmental—they just know that they are right.

So everything that you have done to buy the lie that you are judgmental, when the only person you actually ever judge is you, will you destroy and uncreate all that now, and start coming out of judgment of you? Please. Right and Wrong, Good and Bad, POD and POC, All Nine, Shorts, Boys and Beyonds.™ Thank you.

So, let's say you're walking by somebody who has judgments of their body and you look at their body and perceive all this judgment that the person is inflicting on their body, and that they have of themselves, and you think those are your judgments because you can perceive them. Now, at this point you go; *"Oh, I'm so judgmental of people's bodies. I can't believe I'm judging somebody's body like that!"*

Are you really judging their body or are you aware of their judgments of their body and of the projections of other people placed on their body? And does it mean that you're judgmental, or does it mean that you're actually aware? Get ready to practice being in allowance: Have you ever walked by an obese person and had judgments about the size of their body? Did you then judge yourself for being judgmental?

Here's another thing you normally wouldn't ever think about: Have you ever seen someone you thought was really sexy and that you really wanted to be with them? Of course, right? Have you ever asked, "Is this my point of view? Or am I picking up their projection of what they want me (and usually everyone else) to think about them?"

Try it. You'll be surprised to realize that many people project what they want you to think about them and their bodies.

I had a woman tell me, "I used to wonder how I could be so judgmental when I cared so much about people. It wasn't until I started asking these questions that I realized that, far from being judgmental, I'm really, really aware."

But that's probably not true for you. You're probably as judgmental as you think you are.

(Did that make you feel lighter or heavier? Are you starting to get how this light/heavy thing works???)

So will you please let go of everything you've done to buy that you're judgmental because you can perceive the limitations from which other people function, and always have your whole life? Like where you look and realize, *"That person acts really superior. This one is selfish. This one is unkind to people."* Then you think, *"Oh my God, I'm judging!"* No, you're most likely NOT judging. You're most likely having an awareness of how they're choosing to function in life.

People have asked me, "What if it's just something I want to hear? What if that's why it feels lighter?" Let me give you another, different example.

Several years ago, my friend Gary's mother was in the hospital and was close to dying. One day at lunch he had a weird feeling come over him, and he thought that perhaps his Mom had passed. So he looked down at his watch and saw it was 1:40 p.m. When he asked in his head if she had died, he felt lighter on "yes."

His sister called him a few hours later to let him know his Mom had passed at 1:40 in the afternoon—exactly the time he was at lunch and had that feeling. Even though it wasn't something he necessarily wanted to hear, it made him feel lighter when he asked if his Mom had passed.

That's the level of awareness you can have when you go beyond judgment. Since Gary didn't have to judge if it was good or bad that his mother had died, there was no charge and he could have the awareness that she had with a sense of ease.

⌐ ⌐ ⌐

Wrong—The New Right?

One of the greatest gifts you can give yourself is the willingness to be wrong—without having to judge you for it. Then you can stop trying in vain to prove that you are perfect by having to be right all the time.

Here, let's try something for a moment. It's a tool I got from my friend Gary. Say this out loud, all 10 times.

You're right. I'm wrong.

You're right. I'm wrong.

You're right. I'm wrong.

You're right. I'm wrong.

You're right. I'm wrong.

You're right. I'm wrong.

You're right. I'm wrong.

You're right. I'm wrong.

You're right. I'm wrong.

You're right. I'm wrong.

Do you feel lighter or heavier? For 99% of people, when I have them do this, they feel lighter. Why? Because it's so nice to be able to be willing to be wrong and not to have to prove you are right all the time.

There was a woman who had been doing Access for some time who went to visit her mother at the family home. The normal routine between them was that the mother would have continuous, barb-like, verbal judgments of her daughter for all the things she wasn't doing right (like going to church, getting married, having children, that sort of thing). So she called Gary and asked what she could do. Gary responded, "Tell her, you're right, Mom, I'm wrong. Three times."

The woman said that she couldn't, because she hadn't done anything wrong. Gary said, "I know you haven't done anything wrong. Just say it and see how it goes."

So the woman did. She called Gary, elated. She had done as Gary instructed. And after the third time of saying it, her mom pulled her close and said, "You're not wrong, dear. You're just mistaken."

The woman said that not only was it the first time in the last 10 years that she had a pleasant visit home, but that her mother gave her a $5,000 check when she left! Such is the power of the willingness to be wrong.

You can also use this phenomenal tool to change your relationships. When you have done something that you know has caused an upset with someone you care about, you can say, *"You're right. I'm wrong. What can I do to make up for the damage done?"* If you say this with vulnerability, presence, and total sincerity it can be the catalyst for creating a totally different possibility in your relationship, and it can undo perceived wrongness for both of you.

The only way most people are willing to change something is if they believe that what they are currently choosing is wrong. They are so busy trying to prove they are not wrong, because they already believe they are wrong. So they won't change anything, because if they change anything, it means what they chose in the past was wrong, but they are not willing to be wrong, even though they have considered themselves wrong every moment of their lives.

Does that sound insane to anyone else?

In the Universe there is no "wrong" or "right." It is a constant flow of receiving and gifting. This reality is not. This reality tries to get you to judge everything that's great about you as wrong, so you can fit in and be no greater than "normal."

What if there is a greatness that you are, that is hidden behind every wrongness that you are trying to hide?

What if everything that is wrong with you, or about you, isn't actually wrong? What if it's actually a potency you have that doesn't match this reality, but no one has ever been capable of showing you that?

Will you make the demand that you will actually show you everything that is true for you, even though it may be different than what seems to be true for everyone else? Whatever it looks like? Whatever it takes? You're the only one who can.

It is weird being different. But what if it were fun?

What if it weren't wrongness but simply a difference?

What if the Earth let you come here because of that difference?

What if it *made* you come here because of that difference?

What if *you* made you come here because of that difference?

What if there was everything wrong with you and nothing wrong with you all at the same time?

What if everything that you thought was wrong with you were the space and possibility that you're willing to be that is <u>beyond this reality</u>?

What if it were the kindness, the caring, the gentleness, the loving, the joy, and the awareness of something different that you are that nobody else ever got, and you've decided that it couldn't be and couldn't exist and didn't matter, and only this limited reality did?

What if you could begin to be totally different now? By being you?

Everything that doesn't allow that to show up, will you destroy and uncreate all that now please? Right and Wrong, Good and Bad, POD and POC, All Nine, Shorts, Boys and Beyonds.™

All the changes you've avoided choosing because it meant that somehow you were wrong for what you chose in the past, will you destroy and uncreate all that please, and allow those changes to show up now with ease? Right and Wrong, Good and Bad, POD and POC, All Nine, Shorts, Boys and Beyonds.™ *Thank you.*

How Do You Know?

How do you know if you are judging—or if you are just being aware?

The million dollar question, right?

Look at these sentences: *He is a very attractive man.*
That could be a judgment, right? Or an awareness.

She is a mean woman.
That could also be a judgment. Or an awareness.

So what is the difference?
What is it?

Most people think that if what they are perceiving is "negative," then they are judging. They think that if what they are perceiving is "positive," that they are not judging. Actually, the difference between a judgment and an awareness is the energetic charge on that subject for you—the vibration of your point of view.

It is the energetic charge of a judgment that gets you stuck in polarity of right and wrong, of conclusion and the un-willingness to ask questions and change.

If it is an awareness, you have no charge!

You are willing to change your point of view at any time and you don't have to defend it, hold on to it, or explain it.

In any way.
It is just something you are aware of, in these 10 seconds. *How does it get even lighter than that?*

Who Does This Belong To?

How many times have you perceived the wrongness in other people, the places where they believe they're wrong, perceive they're wrong, can only receive the wrongness of them and know that they are wrong beyond the shadow of a doubt?

How much of your life have you spent believing that the sense of wrongness you perceive is really yours, when in actuality it's what you're aware of in the world around you?

So, truth, is it yours or someone else's? Or a LOT of someone else's?

It feels just like you. Your stomach starts churning, and you feel the rightness buttons kick in where you feel wrong and want to be right and this person is wrong and it feels just like yours....

This is the time to ask this question:

WHO DOES THIS BELONG TO?

Is it mine or someone else's? *If all of a sudden you get lighter, it is because it isn't yours.* It isn't yours, sweet beautiful you. Not yours! You can return it to sender.

Yes! Just return it. Send it back. Away with it. Be gone ... someone else's judgments.

Remember: You can't handle a problem that isn't yours. You can't change a thought, a feeling, or an emotion that isn't yours. But you can do something far easier. You can simply return it to whomever it actually belongs—even when you don't know who that is.

You don't have to do anything about it. You can just return it to its original creator, EVEN IF YOU HAVE NO IDEA WHO THAT IS. Just return it to sender.

If it's not yours, just give it back—with consciousness attached.

You always think, *"Oh my God, that felt just like me."*

You know what? It always feels just like you—because your awareness is that brilliant and that intense and that great. It ALWAYS feels like you, or you would never buy it as yours!

Please get this: 98 percent of all your feelings, emotions and thoughts do not belong to you! They are someone else's. But what you're aware of feels just like you—even though it's not.

The only way you're ever going to tell the difference is by asking the question:

WHO DOES THIS BELONG TO?

Ask it, and if it lightens up at all, it isn't yours.
You, being you, are light.

You trying to be someone else, are heavy.

Way, Way Beyond Your

Body

Would You Be Willing to Try This?

Just put your hands on your face.
Close your eyes.

Feel your hands on your face.
Feel your face in your hands, your hands on your face.

Take a deep breath in.

Notice how it feels to be present with your body.

Connect with your body and say:
"Thank you for you. How much fun can we have today?"

— Chapter 3 —
Your Body Knows

What if you are an infinite being? A being that has the capacity to perceive, know, be and receive EVERYTHING?

Does that feel light to you?

Me too.

I used to get really upset when people in the spiritual world would tell me that I was an infinite being. They would say it as if it was supposed to be the solution to all the problems I was then having. Talk about FRUSTRATING! I used to think: "If I am an infinite being, why can't I get anything right? If I am infinite—why do I have to struggle to even make enough money to pay rent every month?"

What if it's that you just haven't been given the right tools?

What if we have all been entrained to a reality that doesn't work?

What if this is the very first time you have had the chance to actually claim and acknowledge you?

As the infinite being you truly be.
Are you willing?

Everything that doesn't allow that now, will you destroy and uncreate all that please? Right and Wrong, Good and Bad, POD and POC, All Nine, Shorts, Boys and Beyonds.™

A Pebble in the Ocean

Whenever you feel dynamically, extremely, intensely impacted by anything, you're not occupying enough space. When we try to figure something out, we get real close to our bodies. Too close.

If you were to expand out 100,000 or 200,000 miles in all directions and stay there, instead of trying to come in close to your body to figure out all of the thoughts, feelings and emotions, they would be like a pebble in the ocean.

A pebble has very little impact on the ocean, right? But if you drop a pebble in a thimble it has a big impact. Unfortunately, what you've been doing is making yourself into a thimble energetically rather than being the ocean that you could choose to be.

That's one of the greatest single things we do to limit ourselves continuously: We act like we're small … when we are really, really BIG. Let's start by clearing one thing up once and for all:

You are not your body.
You are an infinite being, not a body.
You are so much bigger than your body.

Would you like me to show you?

Right now, take a moment, close your eyes, and go out and touch the outside edges of you.

Not your body, but you, the being.

Now go 100 yards further, in all directions.

Are you there too?

Now go 100 miles further, in all directions....

Are you there too?

Now go 1,000 miles further in all directions.

Are you there too?

Now go 100,000 miles further in all directions.

Are you there too?

Did you notice that no matter where I asked you to go, there you were?

Could a being that big fit inside of a body as small as yours?

Hint: NO!

So, would you consider a totally different possibility?

You are not your body. You are an infinite being. Your body is your body. You are you. You should have a connection (a great connection, actually). But you are not one and the same.

If you try to jam a being that big into a body this small, it hurts.

Are you actually creating pain and suffering in your body because you're trying to jam yourself into it, because you believe you're only as big as your body? And are you validating other people's realities that you're only that big?

Will you destroy and uncreate all that now please? Right and Wrong, Good and Bad, POD and POC, All Nine, Shorts, Boys and Beyonds.™

What if there were a totally different way of being with your body?

❧ ❧ ❧

Your Body Has Its Own Point of View. You Have Yours.

It's this weird thing—your body has a consciousness of its own. Science tells us that every molecule has consciousness, and every atom. When you put them together in the shape of a body, it still has consciousness.

Everything you've done to totally negate and ignore the fact that your body has its own points of view, its own consciousness, its own awareness, and its own ability to change things, regardless of your attempts to get in the way, will you give all that up and destroy and uncreate it please? Right and Wrong, Good and Bad, POD and POC, All Nine, Shorts, Boys and Beyonds.™

The first step in actually developing a different possibility with your body is to start communicating with it. Begin by asking your body for everything that concerns it.

Have you ever been in a relationship where you just ignored each other and didn't talk to each other? Was it any fun? When that person came to you and asked for a favor, did you really want to give it or no?

It is the same thing with your body!

So, will you please allow yourself to develop a great relationship with your body? How? Start asking your body for everything that concerns it. When you are giving your body what it wants, it feels at ease and peace. And when you're doing that, it will give you what you desire. Really.

If you want to change something, then ask your body, what's it going to take to change this? So rather than, *"Oh my God, I can't believe that my butt is so big!"* Ask: *"Body, what's it going to take to have the firm, petite, beautiful little booty that I'd really like to have? Body, what can we do to change this?"*

Your body will tell you. Of course, you could also destroy and uncreate everything that doesn't allow it to change, but that would make it too easy. The many, many people that have already done this have reported that it actually works!

Continue asking your body for everything that concerns it.

Body, what would you like to eat? Body, whom would you like to eat?
Body, what kind of movement would you like to do?
Body, what kind of clothes would you like to wear?
Body, what kind of person would be fun to have sex with?

⸙ ⸙ ⸙

Conscious Eating

Let's look at the first question: Body, what would you like to eat?

At a restaurant, close your eyes, open the menu, look down, and then open your eyes. The first thing upon which your eyes focus is what your body would like. How do you know you've ordered the right thing? It will be light when you order it and orgasmic when you eat it!

Then eat the first three bites of each thing on your plate in total consciousness.

So in other words, you take a bite in total awareness of where and how it activates every taste bud on your tongue.

Just take a moment, put it in your mouth and only eat what feels truly orgasmic.

That is what your body likes.

Once you get it, you'll know, and it will be difficult to eat anything your body doesn't like.

Is it possible you're going to screw up lots of times and not get it exactly "right?" Very possible! What if that were OK?

∞ ∞ ∞

Practice Body Whispering

Understanding your body's communication is something you get a little bit over time. What is required is practice. You're literally learning a new energetic language. Your natural tendency is to judge you as wrong, as bad, and as though you're not getting it. So, start acknowledging the little successes.

I tried this during one of the first Access classes I ever attended. I was at lunch and asked my body what it wanted to eat. I was getting a salad with my meal, and the waitress asked if I wanted Thousand Island, Ranch, Bleu Cheese, Honey Mustard, or Italian?

My body went *"yummy"* on Honey Mustard. Something went "yummy," though I can't really describe it in words. Let's say it felt slightly more peaceful. But my point of view was "*I like Ranch*," so I asked for Ranch.

I got the salad and it had Honey Mustard on it. Apparently, my body bypassed me and went straight to the waitress' body and got what it wanted. So I tasted it, put it in my mouth, and it was one of the yummiest things I've ever had. Totally orgasmic! Honey Mustard dressing!?!?! And I didn't like Honey Mustard dressing! My body was like: "*I do! And I'm the one eating*!!"

So what you have to get is your body is the one eating, your body is the one copulating, your body is the one moving, your body is the one that has clothes—**not you**.

Being Totally Grateful for This Beautiful Body of Yours

How often do you choose to be gentle and kind and scrumptious with your body?

The difficulty is, once again, in validation of other people's realities around embodiment, you ignore your body, you kick it to the curb, and come back and pick it up when you're ready … but otherwise you ignore it and don't ever talk to it.

What about being grateful for your body exactly as it is right now? What about that? If you'd like to change something about it, then say: *"Body, I didn't know what it was like to be grateful for you, and I'm sorry, and from this space I'd like to change some things. Is that possible?"*

Does that feel any different? Is that a completely different kind of relationship than most people have with their bodies?

How many people on this planet are happy in their bodies? Just look out the window right now if you can—how many people out there do you see that enjoy their bodies? Not many, unfortunately….

༝ ༝ ༝

Do You Ever Judge Your Body? Just a Little?

Do you ever wake up and start your day with a litany of judgment as you stand in front of the mirror? I know you don't like to admit it, you being all conscious and aware and spiritual and all … But have you ever? Just checking. With your body, you always get more of what you judge as wrong.

"These are starting to sag, God, I thought I had more here, and this is starting to get gray, and these are too small and they're getting saggy, and … Oh let's not even talk about that!"

Now ... how many people have "normal" bodies? Is there such a thing as a normal body? Really? Truth?

The standard of what was normal and desirable 100 years ago is different than it is today. Over the years, the plumper version of bodies for the longest time was the most valuable. That meant you were healthy; it meant you had enough food to eat. You weren't "one of them skinny rail-like people that's about to die or blow over in the wind" because of not having enough food. So the standards change over the years. What is a standard?

Judgment—a continuous series of judgments.

Would you be willing to stop validating everybody else's reality about what bodies should look like? Would you be willing to start honoring your own point of view? Your body's? Everything that doesn't allow that, will you destroy and uncreate that please? Right and Wrong, Good and Bad, POD and POC, All Nine, Shorts, Boys and Beyonds.™ Thank you.

Everything you've done to create the litany of judgment of your body as the way to start your day, will you destroy and uncreate all that now please? Right and Wrong, Good and Bad, POD and POC, All Nine, Shorts, Boys and Beyonds.™ Thank you.

❧ ❧ ❧

What Does Your Body DESIRE to Look Like?

Your body has a point of view about what it desires to look like. If you're trying to impose something based on your decisions and judgments—are you two ever going to meet? If your body wants to look one way and it's heading in that direction, and you want it to look another way, and you are trying to make it head in that direction, what occurs right in between those two? That's where the space of judgment occurs.

What if you could drop your point of view and just be grateful for your body as it is? What else might be possible from there? Would that potentially be a source for greater gratitude for being alive? For you? For your sweet body?

Everything that doesn't allow that to show up, will you destroy and uncreate all that now please? Right and Wrong, Good and Bad, POD and POC, All Nine, Shorts, Boys and Beyonds.™ Thank you.

✄ ✄ ✄

Snowball of Judgment

Some years ago, a cover of *Time Magazine* said:
"Why DNA Is Not the Determination of Your Body."

Wait a minute! They've been telling us that it is your DNA that decides everything! What if it isn't? What if that weren't the case? What if it's actually something completely different?

Instead of not being able to change, what if we can actually change our bodies by functioning differently energetically?

You and your body are energetic by your very nature.

What do I mean?

Let's look at one of those days when you start the day with judgment. You know what I mean, right? It's when you wake up and feel like your head is wedged in the south end of a northbound elephant—and the elephant is now sitting on your head.

You start with judgment, and it's like a big black snowball that grows and grows and grows and makes you heavier and heavier ... That's a particular energy, right?

Now, on the other hand, have you had one of those days in your life when you woke up and everything was beautiful and amazing and phenomenal, and you didn't start with judgment? You started instead with a question or a possibility in your head? A question like, *"Wow, how does it get any better than this?"* or, *"What else is possible?"* Instead of adding to judgment, you started adding to possibilities.

Is that a different energy than the first example? Of course.

We literally learn to enforce judgment on us and on our bodies. What if you could wake up and live your life and create your body more from that second energy than from the first? What if that were a possibility? What if it's just that nobody every told you that you could function from there? If you chose to, would your body feel different? Would your life? Which would you rather choose?

Everything that doesn't allow you to create and generate a life and living filled with that second energy (as in all the projections, expectations, separations, judgments and rejections that it's not possible), will you destroy and uncreate all that now please? Right and Wrong, Good and Bad, POD and POC, All Nine, Shorts, Boys and Beyonds.™ Thank you.

∽ ∽ ∽

Even Science Knows This....

Here's another interesting thing that science has known for a long time; **any time you look at a molecule or an atom, you change it.** Your consciousness interacts with the consciousness of the atom, the molecule or the subatomic particle, and changes it.

What if the idea that you couldn't change your body was just a lie that was inflicted upon you? What if it were just a lie you bought from someone a long time ago, and what if you didn't have to have it anymore? If you can change one atom, shouldn't you be able to change more than one ... like those in your body?

Because if you're truly an infinite being, then everything about you that seems like a limitation has its root in a lie. No limitation is infinite—or put another way—all limitation is finite. Does that make sense?

❦ ❦ ❦

Is Pain Real?

One of your body's last resorts for getting your attention is creating pain. That's the one thing it knows you will listen to. It's tried the whisper, the feather touch, and the hand brushing across your face....

Finally it says: *"Hey! I haven't been able to get you to listen any other way. You didn't listen to the pleasure, because you don't believe that exists anymore. You didn't listen to the other really cool feeling I gave you to let you know something else was going on. So now it's pain. Try to avoid that! Stupid being—supposedly really conscious—dumb idiot!"*

See, your body is a sensate, sensational, sensory organism designed to give you information all the time! When it can't get through, it starts screaming—which we interpret as pain. That's your body talking. Your body has had enough of you not listening to it. It has been trying to give you information from day one, and you always interpret it as, *"Oh my God, I feel this way. This hurts!"*

What you ask:

"Hey body, what are you communicating here that I'm not getting? And please give it to me in a way that I can easily get it, because I'm not very bright."

Every feeling is an awareness you're unwilling to have.

"No, it's a feeling! I promise! It's intense!"

Of course it is. You are correct. It is definitely real. What if it were an intensity of awareness? What if it's intense because it's an awareness that you are really intensely aware of? Is that a possibility?

Just try it. *Check—is it light to you?*

❧ ❧ ❧

Hold onto Your Seat! I'm Going to Confuse You a Bit.

There are some other possibilities that require you to ASK A QUESTION.

By now you should be aware: There are ALWAYS other possibilities and more questions to ask. How does it get any better than that?

(Please don't throw the book across the room. Sweet, sweet book. Just scream. That usually works.)

So I have said before that 98 percent of your thoughts, feelings, and emotions don't belong to you.

Now get this: Somewhere between 50 and 100 percent of what goes on in your body doesn't belong to you either!

Ask: *"Is this mine, someone else's or something else?"*

One of those will feel lighter to you. That's the awareness of the "answer" you're looking for. Now, move on to some more questions....

1. If you get lighter on "Is this mine?" ask:

What awareness am I not willing to have here?
Then just stop, and listen.
Quite important this: **You stop and listen.**

Give your body a chance to tell you.

What awareness are you not willing to have here?

2. If you get lighter on "Is it someone else's?" please return it to sender!

Just ask to "return to sender" and then make the demand that you let go of every place where you have bought it as yours. Then POD and POC it. (POD and POC is just the short form of *Right and Wrong, Good and Bad, POD and POC, All Nine, Shorts, Boys and Beyonds.*™)

Why? Because if it is someone else's, you can't do anything about it.

Please know that your body will tell you everything that is going on with all the bodies around it. All the time.

So, if your shoulder starts hurting, what you want to do is ask a question: *"What is going on here, body? Is this mine, someone else's, or something else?"*

Let me give you some examples:

At work

One lady used "Who does this belong to?" and "Is this mine?" every time she had a craving for donuts at work. Within 6 weeks, she had lost 20 pounds, because she had been eating donuts for everyone else at work. With this one question, she eliminated her donut cravings and 20 pounds by just not eating for everyone else.

In my practice

Way back in early 2000 when I was first exposed to this tool, it changed my life, and it also changed my chiropractic practice. Using this tool, I found that I could create a change in 50%–90% of the problems in people's bodies that I had not been able to change previously. Literally. In fact, this tool became so important to my practice that I found myself using it in about 95% of the sessions I was doing. It created results that surprised me utterly.

I had one woman come to me who had tremendous pain in her left knee. She had already had surgery in her right knee and was coming to me because she had just injured her left knee in a similar fashion and was hoping for some relief in the level of pain.

After 20 minutes of work, using primarily the, "Who does this belong to?" tool, her pain level had decreased by 80%. After another 40 minutes of working together, she reported that 99% of the pain was gone. And it never came back!

I'm not saying that this is the case with all knee pain, but it was in this particular case. Having this tool, and the willingness to use it, saved this woman from a lot of pain and created the awareness in her world that what she thought had to be so (living with knee pain) wasn't necessarily so.

In the supermarket

A man who had taken an Access class and gotten this information was walking through a supermarket. He walked by this older woman who asked him to bend down and pick up a roll of toilet paper because she said her back hurt. Without thinking, he asked her, "Who does that belong to?" She said, "My husband." And instantly, she bent down and picked up the toilet paper. Strange, and true.

At the gym

I used to go to the gym and work out all the time, because I had huge judgments of my body. So I'd be working out a lot. I used to weigh 25 pounds more than I do now, and I had 3% less body fat. I was HUGE. And it didn't matter how much I worked out, I still felt really bad about my body.

After starting Access, I went to work out one day. I went in feeling really great about my body, really great about myself, and as soon as I stepped past the threshold of the gym, all of these points of view entered my head: *'Oh my God, my body sucks, my biceps are too small, I haven't done enough, I need to eat better, I need to cut out fat, I need to stop eating Big Macs® and Coke®."* I went, *"Wow, I suck."*

So I asked this question:

Who does this belong to? Is it mine?

And it went whoosh, away. Instantly. It wasn't even mine. I have to tell you, I thought it was weird, too! I thought it was too easy, too! The fact is, it just worked. It totally surprised me.

You are like a big psychic radio receiver, you're picking up this crap all the time from everybody else around you, and everybody is picking it up from everybody else and sharing it around....

What if there were only one person thinking on the planet and everyone else is just picking it up?

How much of the pain and suffering that you believe has been in your body actually isn't yours? Instead, is it your body giving you awareness of the pain, suffering and judgments of other people?

Would you be willing to look at that now? Would you please start asking:

"Is this mine, someone else's or something else?"

So here we go ... Number three.

3. If you get lighter on "Is it something else?" that means it is the Earth's!

The Earth is asking for your assistance in facilitating it. And just like your body, the only way the Earth knows of getting your attention is by giving you pain.

You (Yes, YOU!) have capacities for facilitating the earth, and your body has capacities for facilitating the Earth. If you don't use it when the Earth asks for it, your body will start hurting.

As an example, after the Fukushima earthquake in 2011 and its subsequent radiation spill, I had many people calling me with chest problems. The only thing that began to alleviate the coughing was asking them these questions and then acknowledging that their bodies were contributing to trying to change the problems that were occurring for the Earth and the oceans and the people affected by the radiation.

Yes, you can now call the little men in white coats. Call me silly, call me crazy. It REALLY surprised me, too, when I first came across this information, and it WORKED to change people's symptoms. I know there are many of you out there who would say it was a "placebo" effect, or you'd chalk it up to some sleight of hand.

On the other hand, there are probably many of you reading this who are right now acknowledging, *"Oh my God, I'm not crazy! Someone else has put into words what I've known about for years."* And it's for you that this book was written. Closed-minded people do not change the world. They keep perpetrating everything here that maintains limitation. The cow people of the world have been getting away with making the rest of us wrong for far too long.

And from my point of view, it's time for the dreamers like you that truly desire to change the world to have the tools to do it—no matter how weird it may seem at first.

How many pains, stiffnesses or check-outs do you currently have in your body that are actually from the Earth—or the people on it—demanding or requiring your assistance? Everything that allows that to stay stuck, will you destroy and uncreate it and let it go now please? Right and Wrong, Good and Bad, POD and POC, All Nine, Shorts, Boys and Beyonds.™

The Earth has been gifting to us all for thousands of years. Is now the time to start receiving it?

And gifting back?

Practice with Your Body

Knowing what your body truly desires takes practice.

Remembering to ask your body takes practice.

And finding out what to ask also takes practice.

Did you know that it takes a huge amount of the energy in your food to simply digest it? That you're getting energy from your food is a bit of a lie. You and your body actually require much less food than we have been taught.

For the next couple of days, would you be willing to play at asking some questions every time you "feel" hungry without bothering to try to get it right?

Start with yes and no questions—it's easier. Please know, the answer you get "lighter" on, is the one that is true for your body. Here are some examples:

Body....

Do you require something? Yes/No
Is that yours or another body's?

Do you require food? Yes/No
If yes, is that yours or another body's?

Do you require something to drink? Yes/No
Is that yours or another body's?

Is there anything in the fridge you desire? Yes/No
Is that yours or another body's?

Do you require ... broccoli ... ? Yes/No
(Please put in whatever you are considering to eat.) Is that yours or another body's?

Would you like something else? Yes/No
Is that yours or another body's?

Do you require movement? Yes/No
Is that yours or another body's?

Do you require being touched? Yes/No
Is that yours or another body's?

Do you require sex? Yes/No
Is that yours or another body's?

Please know: We often eat to avoid BEING THE SPACE we truly be, and the lightness we truly be. We don't recognize that space as us, so we perceive it as a wrongness and do everything to come back to the heaviness that is more familiar to us. In this case, by eating.

But what if what you BE is SPACE? And lightness?

Everything you've done to eat to avoid being the space of you, or to fill up being the space of you, by eating, or by any other means, will you please destroy and uncreate all that? Right and Wrong, Good and Bad, POD and POC, All Nine, Shorts, Boys and Beyonds.™ Thank you.

Starting to

Receive

Asking the Chair

I would like to take a moment to show you
something....

So what would it be like right now if you asked the
consciousness of the chair that you are sitting on to make your body more
comfortable?

Ask.
Did it get more comfortable?
For most people it does.

Is that weird or what?
Are you wishing someone had told you that before?

Consciousness is part of everything. Even though you usually don't want to
know it, you are actually oneness with everything.

You are that space between the molecules (and atoms) of your body. The
part of the atom that appears solid is only 0.0001 percent of the whole
atom.

The rest is space and possibility and consciousness ... You....

*What if the space between the molecules and consciousness of your body is the same as the
space between the molecules of the chair?*

Which is the same as the space between the molecules of the air.

Which is the same as the space between the molecules of the walls.

*Which is the same as the space between the molecules of
the building.*

*Which is the same as the space between the molecules of the street, and the
earth around you and the entire solar system, the entire galaxy, and the
entire Universe.*

What does that mean?

It means that you are way larger, way more connected, way more in
connection and communion with
everything, and have way more options than you
have acknowledged. Ever.

Ever.

And if you allow it, that connection and communion, could lead to more
ease than you ever imagined possible....

— Chapter 4 —
Ask and You Shall Receive

What is your point of view of this world? Is there enough for everyone? Enough food? Enough money? Enough love? Enough space? Enough joy? Or is there a limited amount, so that if you, for example, have love, someone else has to do without?

Would you please look at this for a moment?

Your point of view creates your reality. Reality does not create your point of view. So if you have the point of view that we live in a universe of lack and scarcity, what reality are you creating?

My point of view and my knowing is that we live in a universe of total abundance. The Bible was right about one thing: *Ask and you shall receive.* Isn't it weird—you just ask and you receive?

But how? If there is a how, it is just to be present in your life and be willing to receive the energies of another possibility. When being the totality of receiving, you let all your barriers down and receive everything. No exclusion. In ease, joy and glory, you receive the good, the bad and the ugly.

Now, here is a little difficulty for many of us....

If we ask for a million dollars today, and it doesn't show up tomorrow, we go, *"Oh, the Universe does not work, I'm so wrong, I'm doing this wrong."*

But what has to happen is the Universe literally has to rearrange itself for you to have what you've asked for. That's what it's doing from the moment you ask. Yet, what happens is when it doesn't show up, then we go into, *"Oh it's not showing up"*—and then it stops, of course, because we decided and concluded that it isn't. That point of view creates the reality that shows up.

We've shouted our conclusion out into the Universe: "It's not showing up!" and the Universe listens and nicely, politely obeys.

Instead we could be asking (those darn questions again):
"Is it actually showing up in a totally different way than I could ever imagine? How does it get even better than that?"

Please get this my beautiful friends ...

It is always going to look different than the way you thought it was going to. Always!

The way you thought it was going to look was based on all your judgments about what it should look like, not based on awareness of what it could look like, because your judgments of what it should look like kept you from being aware of what it could look like. And all those points of view of what it should look like are precisely why it could not show up before now.

Are you with me? Wanna read that one again?

What about YOU starting to receive? Yes, my dear—you.

What do you long for? To be seen? To be heard? To be received, in totality? Oh yes! I can hear you in my head:

"Of course, dumb question. If you just receive me, then all will be good; I will be validated and valuable. Then I will exist."

Here comes my question. I think I will whisper at first:

What about receiving? Louder?

WHAT ABOUT RECEIVING?

"Oh, I receive," you say. "Of course I do. I mean, receiving is no problem.
If someone wants to give something to me, I receive, of course I do. I love
receiving, no, no, no, I have no problem receiving."

Anyone else who feels a bit heavy? Most people don't receive much on this planet. Have you noticed? Whether you believe it or not, that goes for many of you who are reading this book right now.

Just look at this for a second, please:

You were always the most capable one around, who tried to prove that you weren't. But you always knew that nobody had as much capacity as you, so you've always been the one that was always willing to be on your own, and do everything on your own, even while thinking you needed other people, which you rarely do.

That doesn't allow much receiving. What it does allow for is a lot of control and a lot of attempted force to try to create things into existence.

Receiving is a totally different ball game.

As an example, let's say you live in a small little country up in northern Europe. Half of the year it is pitch black and cold as hell. Let's call the country, Sweden, just for fun.

Now imagine you wake up and it is the **first day of spring,**
in Sweden.

What is that like?

After 6 months of darkness, are you more alive than any time in the frigging Universe ever or what? You think, *"Oh, Sun ... Sun. Wow!"*

You go out in the zero degree weather, drinking cappuccinos, with your face turned up towards the bleak sun, smiling. It's so cold, you can see your breath ... and who cares? You made it through another winter! That's the feeling of: *"Oh my God, I am alive! Bring it on baby, bring everything on! I am hot!"*

Now contrast that with **a morning in the middle of winter.**

You wake up and you think, *"Why do I have to be here? Can I hit the snooze alarm 27 more times? Can I call in sick today? No, it is my own business. The owner is going to know I am lying."*

And when you walk out of your house, you don't want anyone to see you, or talk to you. You are having a really bad hair-day.

Notice those are two totally different ways of being in the world? Which one would you rather have more of?

The first one is infinite receiving. With the first energy, you can receive all the money, people, love, sex and relationship you could ever desire.

Yet the other is the one we tend to choose a lot more often, the point of view of: *"No, I am not going to receive anything from anyone. I am in my own little bubble, and that is it. I will hold on here, and put this barrier up here, and then this one here, and then totally shut off my body and face. So there ... I am safe."*

There isn't much receiving going on in this reality. Actually, this reality is dedicated to the total exclusion of it. Everything here is based on *"If I give you this, what do I get?"* and *"If I accept this, what do I have to give you?"*

There is an alternative. As an infinite being—which is what you truly be—you can receive everything. Everything! Did that feel any lighter? The thing is ... You have to CHOOSE it.

Everything that doesn't allow you to choose it, will you please destroy and uncreate it all now? Right and Wrong, Good and Bad, POD and POC, All Nine, Shorts, Boys and Beyonds.™

Oh, by the way, there's no such thing as a money issue. All money "issues" are created by what you are unwilling to receive.

ॐ ॐ ॐ

One of my greatest teachers

In this reality, you have to keep reminding yourself to choose to receive. It's not something we do because it is not something we are taught.

Let me tell you a little story. I have a horse that is one of the most phenomenal beings I have ever come across. His name is Playboy.

He's an ex race-horse, and he used to belong to my friend, Gary. Since I was not a good rider at the time I met Gary (and Playboy), I had never even thought of riding him. Yet, he would run around in the place where Gary kept his horses, stop at me, and bow his head. Then he would run for a while more, come back and bow his head again—directly in front of me.

Gary tried to sell him, but all the sales fell through. Finally we were out trail-riding one day, and I asked, *"Gary, can I ride him?"*

We were far away from civilization, out on this trail. And Playboy usually would run away with anyone on his back. Given my novice rider status, Gary was a bit hesitant to allow me to ride him. OK, he was really hesitant, but he finally gave in and said yes.

So I climb on, and I've got the reins practically dropping down to the ground, so I have no control on the horse's mouth at all.

Playboy looks up at me and he goes, *"My man."* I look down at him and think, *"My horse."*

I kick him into a canter and we go bloopedy, bloopedy, bloopedy, bloop … It was a small, sweet, smooth canter where he was totally taking care of me. At one point we are going around this turn, and I am starting to fall out of the seat. Playboy moves his butt under me, so he doesn't lose me. Amazing horse. Amazing being.

For my part, I had tears rolling down my face as we rode. It was unlike anything I had ever experienced before, and I'm not even quite sure how to put it into words.

Imagine having someone that you know you can trust totally peer into your soul and totally acknowledge every aspect of you as a being—with absolutely no judgment and no projection of wrongness. It was like being totally loved, totally cared for, totally acknowledged, and not judged to such a degree that it exploded all judgment out of my world. All thought vanished. All needs disappeared.

I now know that I had an experience of Be-ing that day. I had an experience of Oneness, where everything exists and nothing is judged. But it wasn't just tears and space. IT WAS FUN! It was intense!

It was like riding a rocket of non-judgment to a Universe of simply, intensely, spaciously, non-judgmentally, joyfully Be-ing. I don't know HOW it occurred (nor do I care). I just know THAT it occurred.

This is what I've come to know is possible as our lives and in connection with those things in the Universe that desire to gift to us. All it requires is that we choose it—**and be willing to receive it**—and then allow it to show up.

Everything that doesn't allow that to show up for you, STARTING NOW, will you destroy and uncreate all that please? Right and Wrong, Good and Bad, POD and POC, All Nine, Shorts, Boys and Beyonds.™ Thank you.

Yet, even with that communion Playboy and I had—and have—for the longest time I wasn't willing to receive from him, not in totality. There was always some part of me I kept separate, as though that was the only way to have me as I had defined me. I'm sure you're not doing that anywhere in your life, are you???

A couple of years ago he got cancer. With my travel schedule, and with my refusal to receive from him, he decided he would rather get out than live the life he was living.

See, he won't let anybody else ride him. He is my horse, and I am his man. That's it. One time after becoming my horse, Playboy let Gary ride him to show me how to ride a certain way. He took Gary three times around the ring and then stopped. It was as if he was telling Gary. *"You can get off now. Let Dain back on."*

So when Playboy got cancer, I and a few other people asked him, *"Is there anything that we can do here?"* He said: *"Yeah, I would really like Dain to ride me once a week. But I will let the trainer ride me once a week if Dain rides me once a month."* I went, *"Okay done."*

He said, *"Oh and one other thing, you have to start receiving from me or I am out of here."* Only I didn't exactly know what he meant at the time. So, having access to the tools I do, I used one of them. **I ASKED TO BE SHOWN what he meant, since I had no clue.**

Shortly after that, I left for a trip to Europe. I was doing session after session, after meeting, after session, after meeting, after class, after class, after meeting, after session, after meeting, and so on. I wasn't listening to my body, and I was getting sick. I usually function like the sun, a six-year-old, and the Energizer bunny put together in some strange way—and just because you can do that, it doesn't mean it is your best option.

My body was telling me, loud and clear, what was required. I had to start receiving. As in putting down all my barriers and receiving from my horse, from the Earth, from the people and everything else around me that were willing to gift to my body and me.

I laid in my bed, put my hands on my body, and talked to my horse. I know it sounds really funny. But I did, and I was like, *"Okay Playboy, you obviously have something to gift me, what is it that I've been refusing to receive?"* And then I POC and POD'd everything that didn't allow me to receive whatever it was.

This energy of being and presence and kindness and caring and gentleness and joy of embodiment filled my body and I went, *"Oh sh*t, this is what I have been refusing for the last 8 years!?!?!"*

Refusing.

I have been working on receiving continuously for the last 10 years in all the things that I have done. It is all about receiving more, knowing more, being more and perceiving more.

Still I didn't realize how much I was still refusing to receive.

Is it possible that there is something (or maybe a lot of things) you are still refusing to receive?

Would you be willing to stop refusing? Right now?
From the Universe?
From those around you that truly desire to gift to you?
From me?

Even if you don't know what it looks like or what it takes?

Everything that doesn't allow that, will you please destroy and uncreate all that? Right and Wrong, Good and Bad, POD and POC, All Nine, Shorts, Boys and Beyonds.™
Thank you.

The Universe Has Your Back

Would you be willing to start every morning by asking this question:

Who am I today and what grand and glorious
adventures am I going to have and RECEIVE today?

What would it take to have what you desire in life? Don't look for an answer; *just receive the energy of it.* Now ask yourself if you are willing to receive without preconceiving what you would have to receive in order to have what you desire?

Are you willing to receive without projections,
expectations, separations, conclusions, judgments,
rejections or answers of what that has to be or how it has
to look?

Everything that doesn't allow that, will you please destroy and uncreate all that now?
Right and Wrong, Good and Bad, POD and POC, All Nine, Shorts, Boys and
Beyonds.™ Thank you.

What is truly possible for you then? What would you change if you knew that the Universe were on your side?

Because it is. **The Universe is totally on your side.** It has your back.

Deep down you know that. You've always known that. (Even if it has been hidden deep down in some obscure, rarely travelled, sparsely furnished, never-ending corridor of you.)

Would you be willing to start receiving the energy of that KNOWING now?

Everything that doesn's allow that, let's uncreate and destroy that now.

1 ... 2 ... 3! Right and Wrong, Good and Bad, POD and POC, All Nine, Shorts, Boys and Beyonds.™

The Universe has your back. IT desires to gift to you. Yes, you.

What if There Were Something Right About Everything You've Chosen?

Perhaps you are contemplating stopping reading now.

If that is what you choose, go for it!

What if there were something right about everything you have ever chosen?

What if it were exactly the right thing for you, to stop reading right here?

I have no point of view.
I know you think I do. But I don't.

The cool thing is, you can choose to start reading at any point again, maybe in 10 years, maybe tomorrow.

How does it get any better than that?

You can even shred this book, and still choose to pick up THE ENERGY OF IT at another point of time in your life.

Now, how does it get even weirder than that?

Potency of

Caring

What if We're All Sleeping Giants?

What if we've got this AMAZING potency and capacity—and it just looks totally different than the way we thought it was going to?

What if your greatest potency is not the force and the meanness and the anger you can deliver?

What if your greatest potency is the gentleness that you can be, the kindness you can be, the caring you are, and the space of infinite allowance you be?

Are you aware that if you choose to be that, it doesn't allow judgment to exist?

Does that sound more like you?

What if we're all sleeping giants? **Yes, you too.**

Please ask this question everyday:

If I were truly caring for me and the world today, what would I choose right away?

Your life will change.

— Chapter 5 —
What if Caring Were the Core of You?

Take my hand and let me lead you down memory lane for a moment ...
You are a teenager again ... a body that doesn't quite fit ... words that won't
come out right ... and a constant simmering boil of feelings and emotions.
Those glorious years of total bliss, ease and joy we all have experienced....

Do you remember these three words, "I don't care."

Pick one of the many times you uttered them to yourself, to your friends,
parents, teachers, a cute boy, cute girl, rejecting you, again....

Was it true that you didn't care? Of course not.

You cared far more than you would ever admit—even to yourself.

We all know that about teenagers.

What if that is still true?

What if you care far more than you've ever wanted to know? What if you care far more than you've ever wanted to acknowledge to anyone, including you? And how much have you decided that it's that caring that has gotten you into trouble? That your intense caring is what makes you weak? And is responsible for your hurting and your pain?

My friend, it's not your caring that's responsible for your hurting and your pain. It's where you cut off your caring—for you and them—that causes hurting and pain.

Our caring for other people is always the first thing we try to cut off when we think somebody is trying to hurt us.

It feels easier to judge someone and think about what they did wrong (so you can be justified in not being close to them) than it does to put down your barriers and say, *"You know what, it's really tough to say, but I just adore you. I like you so much, and it hurts so much that you don't want me to be as close as I want to be with you. That's really what's going on, which is why I try to judge you, and make you wrong, and try to separate from you."*

Have you ever tried to tell somebody that? What would happen? All their circuits would fry; they would look at you like you were from another planet. And they would quite possibly melt—into the softness they've always wanted to be that they never felt safe to be.

Unfortunately, nobody else does that here. It's not because we can't, it's because we've learned not to. We feel like we can't care for people who are choosing not to receive it. The problem is, you already do care, and you can't stop. You're buying a lie when you think, "Oh, I don't care about them."

Who are you killing when you do that? You. You just stopped caring for you by buying the lie that you can cut off your caring for anybody else. In order to try to stop caring for them, you can only do it by cutting off your caring for everyone, which includes YOU. And … it doesn't work anyway!

What if you didn't? What if your point of view was, *'No matter what, I'm still going to care for me. And I'm still going to care regardless of what the people around me choose.'* That's the only way you will allow yourself to have the joy of your reality—by being willing to actually care as much as you truly do, and not cut it off—regardless of what anyone else chooses.

Because that actually involves caring for you.

Everything you've done to try to prove to you that you don't care, and to not acknowledge how very much you care—even for people that hurt you—will you destroy and uncreate all that please? Right and Wrong, Good and Bad, POD and POC, All Nine, Shorts, Boys and Beyonds.™

✐ ✐ ✐

We are Beings of Oneness

You've got to get over this lie that you don't care at some point, beautiful being. It's not that you're wrong and you're bad for believing you don't care. It is just what you learned from a very young age. It's just what most people choose so that they don't ever have to see how truly different they are and how truly different they'd like the world to be.

Many people have checked out of their entire lives based on this one thing: *Not wanting to acknowledge how much they care and how much people here refuse to receive—and gift—that caring.*

How much caring have you refused to receive?
How much caring have you refused to be?
Will you acknowledge that?
Will you acknowledge that it's not the real you?
And that it's not true for you?

You desire something different.

If not, you wouldn't be reading this book. You desire something other than cutting off your caring so you can stay "in" this reality. You know there is something greater possible.

Will you acknowledge that? Whatever it takes. Will you do that now?

Everything that doesn't allow that, will you destroy and uncreate all that please? Right and Wrong, Good and Bad, POD and POC, All Nine, Shorts, Boys and Beyonds.™

By the way, caring for you and joy go hand in hand. Cutting off from your caring for you and other people doesn't work.

It doesn't work!

We can't do it and maintain joy. We can't do it and have abundance. We can't do it and have connection. We can't do it and create possibilities. Caring is one of the greatest things that is missing in this reality—caring. If everyone on the planet right now had total caring for themselves and each other, would our planet function the way it does? Would it feel the way it does? Would there be genocide? War?

What would it be like if you were to demand that the totality of your caring was going to show up for you, no matter what? Demand it even if it takes a thousand years … a week … or if it manifests right now?

Right now.

And everything that doesn't allow you to receive—and be—the true caring for you that would make it a joy to be alive, will you destroy and uncreate all that please? Right and Wrong, Good and Bad, POD and POC, All Nine, Shorts, Boys and Beyonds.™

☙ ☙ ☙

Did You Learn to Be Upset with People?

Get this: You are oneness (where everything exists and nothing is judged). You are it. When you make your being separate, you cease to exist as you.

And let me tell you, I am still working on this one. I am not the poster boy for consciousness, if that is what you thought.

Let me give you an example, a really silly one, especially when talking about oneness. . . .

I was meeting a friend of mine to have coffee. Then she didn't call. I set aside time, I made plans, and she didn't call. Instead she called the next morning: *"Sorry I didn't call last night. I worked late, and then I was really tired."*

The first thing I wanted to do was go:
"B*TCH! How dare you dishonor my sacred time?!?!"
That was the first place I wanted to go. Then, because it didn't feel good, I asked a question, *"What would MY point of view really be in this situation?"* (Hint: When you're choosing what's true for you, it feels "good" or "light." When you're not choosing what's true for you, it always feels "heavy.") After a few moments, I realized, "This is not me. I am happy for someone to have the choice to do anything they want to do, whether it involves me or not."

Weird. I was surprised at what my actual point of view was. Then I looked over my past and I realized that this had always been my point of view when I was younger, and because of that I WAS TOLD that I didn't care enough.

I was told that I was being walked on—and I bought it.

I was told that people were taking advantage of me. **So I learned to be upset with people. I learned that you couldn't just be kind to people all the time, just because it works for you.** I learned that one has to be upset in the appropriate situations.

Have you learned that too?

Truth?
Does that make you feel lighter?
Does it make you feel more connected to you?

Does it make you feel closer to anybody else?

If the answers to all of the above are 'no' for you too, then perhaps you might consider asking yourself these questions:

Have I been taught to judge as though that is caring?

Have I been taught to judge rather than care?

Have I been taught that separating from others and making them wrong is truly caring for me?

What other choices do I have that would make me feel lighter and happier than those I've been choosing?

There are other choices available that actually involve caring for you. You just have to be willing to choose them. When you're willing to choose them, you'll then be able to see them.

Everything that doesn't allow you to know what those choices are, and actually be able to choose them, will you please destroy and uncreate all that now? Right and Wrong, Good and Bad, POD and POC, All Nine, Shorts, Boys and Beyonds.™

                                      ✺ ✺ ✺

Here's Another Different One for You:
Do you know what is one of the most intimidating things to intimidators?

It is when you're not able to be manipulated into anger, rage, hate, judgment and separation. One of the most intimidating things to people who try to intimidate you is when you do not separate from them no matter what they do. It scares them.

Then they don't know how to manipulate you, and they don't know how to push your buttons.

So, let's go back to when my dear friend calls me after standing me up the evening before. I am supposed to be angry based on everything I've been taught, but I choose differently. I choose to be me. (By the way, this all takes about 10 seconds.) From that place of me, I say: "Hey beautiful, how's it going?"

"Oh great, I am so sorry for not being there last night. I so wanted to see you," she answers.

I could feel my whole being relax. Because that's really what the problem was. I felt hurt because I thought she didn't want to see me. I felt hurt, so I got angry to cover it up so nobody would see that I felt less valuable and less desirable.

I was very grateful that I was able to be that vulnerable with myself and choose differently. I realized then that being that angry didn't work for me. I was not avoiding being angry because it didn't work for her, or because it would be bad for her. It didn't work for me, for who I would like to be.

How many choices are you making that don't really work for you, because it's what you were taught you were supposed to choose? Will you destroy and uncreate all that now please? Right and Wrong, Good and Bad, POD and POC, All Nine, Shorts, Boys and Beyonds.™ *Thank you.*

✌ ✌ ✌

Now for an Even-More-Interesting Point of View: It hurts because they won't receive you.

Please be aware that when somebody is mean to you, it is hurtful because they won't receive you, and they won't receive your caring, and they won't receive their own, and that is hurtful to you.

It is not that they are trying to hurt you. You couldn't care less. It is that you would like to take away the pain and suffering that you perceive in the world. No matter what someone does to you, you still care. No matter whether its abuse or molestation or meanness or judgment or unkindness or stealing or anything else, you still care.

You think you're not supposed to.

As in, *"Oh, they did this wrongness to me, so now I'm supposed to not care about them."* You spend your entire life trying not to care ... but you do. You still do.

So everything you've done to buy that you could stop caring about someone, when you just can't, will you please let that go now? Right and Wrong, Good and Bad, POD and POC, All Nine, Shorts, Boys and Beyonds.™ Thank you.

I am asking that you please be willing to step into no judgment ... where everything is just an interesting point of view. This is also known as allowance, where everything anyone chooses (including you) is just an interesting point of view. Then you can be the difference that will allow things to change.

You care too much and are way too large to exclude anything!

When you do, when you cut people off and pretend you don't care, you also exclude you. *That is why it feels so horrendous.*

Would you be willing to care about you so greatly, and would you be willing to be so different that you became such an intensity of caring and space that you showed the world that it were possible?

What would it be like if you had such an intensity of caring and gratitude that you BECAME IT? Is it possible that you would like to have gratitude and caring for your life and living in every moment? Be grateful for what every moment brought, wherever you were and whomever you were with?

Isn't that what you have been looking for your whole life?
We're taught to not be vulnerable.

We're taught to not care.

We're taught to not be present.

We're taught not to gift.

We're taught to wall ourselves off from everyone and everything and try to control the world around us to try to get our piece before anybody else does—*and for 99% of the people reading this book, it just doesn't work.*

If it doesn't work for you, would you be willing to choose something different now?

What if you, being you, is caring, gratitude, gifting, presence and vulnerability and the difference the world requires?

Just check it out....

∽ ∽ ∽ ∽ ∽ ∽

What if you, being you, is caring, gratitude, gifting, presence and vulnerability?

∽ ∽ ∽ ∽ ∽ ∽

Is it light to you?

Is it true for you?

What do you know?

What would YOU like to choose?

∽ ∽ ∽

Do You Want to Know HOW to Be That?

There is no how.

I know. Irritating.

You just have to make the demand that you be it and then ask a question. (Yes, a question. Again.)

First the demand:

"No matter what it takes I am demanding that I care for me and that I be grateful for me. No matter how long it takes for me to be willing to have that or what it looks like, I am demanding it occur—and it starts now."

Then you ask:

"Hey Universe, what's it going to take? Because I don't know what it is going to take to be in a constant state of gratitude and caring and space because I don't know anybody who lives there and because no one ever taught me how."

You ask the Universe because you don't have a clue. Really, it is not your job to have a clue, sweet beautiful you. Your job is simply to sincerely request that it occurs, and then ask the question.

Then "POC and POD" everything that doesn't allow it to show up:

Everything that doesn't allow this to show up, destroy and uncreate it. Right and Wrong, Good and Bad, POD and POC, All Nine, Shorts, Boys and Beyonds.™

And the Universe hears you and says;

"Yay!!! At last, you asked a question! Whoo-hoo, this is going to be so much fun!!! We can play together now! So I know you have no idea, so check this out: I am going to give you some real easy steps to start with. OK?"

Some days it will be easy, and some days it will be so difficult you will just want to jump off the planet … but now, you are on your way….

Don't give up….
Now is the time….
Just keep asking….
And keep choosing….
And keep moving forward….
And what you are asking for will occur….
(Please … please … no matter what, if you muster up the courage to just keep moving … nothing will ever stop you again … It may slow you down, but it will never truly stop you ever again….)

If I could wish one thing for you—and gift one thing to you—it would be that no one and nothing would ever be able to stop you again from creating the life—and the world—you would truly like to create, have, and be part of.

Everything that doesn't allow that to show up, and everything that's in the way of you receiving it, will you destroy and uncreate all that please? Right and Wrong, Good and Bad, POD and POC, All Nine, Shorts, Boys and Beyonds.™

Not Significant

Let's have a look at some of the times when you think you really couldn't care less....

My question is if you really don't care—or are you just smart enough NOT TO MAKE IT SIGNIFICANT.

What if you are more aware than you've ever acknowledged?

Anything and anyone you make significant sticks you. You have to judge wherever it is good or bad, right or wrong, will stay or go, give or take....

Oh the joy!

You can care deeply, deeply about someone and still not make that person significant in your life.

Caring doesn't equal need. Or significance.

True caring is total freedom.

Asking TRUTH?

Here is one of the simplest tools of Access.

I use it every day—in facilitating classes, managing my business and in my relations.

Here you go:

Do you want be able to hear the lies people say around you?
EVEN WHEN THEY DON'T KNOW THEY
ARE LYING?

Just ask "Truth?" before asking a question.

It can be out loud or in your head. It doesn't matter. You and everyone else in the room will know if the person is lying or not.

Lying to you—and themselves.

It is a very useful little tool.

It contributes greatly to changing the world.

It would be bad if you tried it. It would definitely increase your awareness of what is going on around you and in your life.

And you don't want that. Right?

Phenomenal?

— Relationships —

One of the Big Things . . . .

… we all do is stop ourselves from changing
so we don't lose our connection to other people.

It is one of the greatest limitations that we have
imposed on ourselves. Just be aware of that.

What you might realize is that by choosing to change, you are going to be
an invitation for the people that desire change.

Even if it changes your connection with them.

Notice I am saying change. **It will be different.**
It may or may not mean you lose them.

The people that don't desire change will often just
leave, or make you wrong and separate from you.

The people that truly desire change will not make it your fault. They will
go: *"Wow, what are you doing? You are so different. Can I have some of that?"*

Oh, and you might ponder this:

**Who would you rather play with, and who would you rather
put your time, energy, and attention on?**

**Those that are resistant to you changing—or those that
are inspired by you changing?**

— Chapter 6 —

Are You Willing to Be Different Enough to Have a Great Relationship?

On this planet, we spend a lot—A LOT—of time and energy on love and relationships. We are so cute, we beautiful beings on this planet.

We have so many judgments, conclusions and points of view about what *true love* is, and isn't. Almost all of us are searching for the perfect relationship—even if we pretend we are not.

Yet, the way I see it, there are so many other possibilities of being with each other! So many.

We're just not taught to embrace any of that here—those possibilities are not part of this reality.

What if we could change the whole paradigm of relationship?! What if we could change it to something that really works for all of us? What if it no longer had to be about control and jealousy and envy and right and wrong? What if it could be about the gift we can be to—and for—each other?

Please know, I am not trying to make you wrong.

Ever.

My only intention is to invite you to a completely different way of being.

Only you know if it is light for you.

Only you know if it is true for you.

♫ ♫ ♫

A Totally Different Perspective on Relationship

I personally know how to do relationships really badly. Because of that, I've had to look at this area really dynamically to see what else might be possible.

Let's start with a different definition of relationship. I know it's different. I know, you will probably want to see me as a little weird for this one. Join the club.

I define relationship as: "<u>the degree of distance (or separation) between two objects</u>."

Why? Because, in order for two objects to relate to each other they have to be separate; otherwise, they are in oneness and then they are not in relationship anymore, because they are not separate. Does that make sense?

I have looked and looked and looked at what creates a great relationship and I must tell you, it's not at all what I thought created a great relationship. So, in looking at this area, I realized we do something different than the ideal we all seem to be striving to achieve. Hence, my different definition of the word relationship.

Let me try to explain it....

If we're in relationship we have to be separate and distinct. So, if you have to create something where you're separate and distinct, don't you have to create separation to maintain that?

Here's another weird one: by the very concept of relationship in this reality, you try to have this with ONLY ONE person, which of necessity excludes you, because there's always two people in the relationship. You won't exclude the other person, until you're tired of trying to give and give and give and give and it doesn't work.

Do you know what I mean? You would exclude you more often than you would exclude them. Here's how it usually works:

FIRST:
You see the person that you think you can become one with. For 10 seconds, you see the greatness of each other that is possible. Yay!!!

SECOND:
Ten seconds later you are judging and trying to cut off—and divorce from—every part of you that doesn't match their judgments (or at least, what you think their judgments are).

THIRD:
You separate further and further and further and further, cutting off more and more and more of you to try to match their judgments, while they cut off more and more and more of them to try to match your judgments, and you wonder why things fall apart eventually. They fall apart because neither of you is there as the person you were when you started the relationship!

That is what most relationships are about.

I would like to see it be different, too. That's why I am presenting you with this different way of looking at this particular area.
I KNOW we can choose to create something different!

But in order for that to occur, we have to acknowledge what is present now and what we are creating now. We have to acknowledge where we are—even if it seems difficult, painful, or impossible to change—if we are ever to get to someplace different.

✑ ✑ ✑

Do You Know Anyone That Has a Truly Caring and Great Relationship?

Truth? Think of it for a second. Do you? If so, you are lucky. Did you know that 90 percent of people would rather have a bad relationship than no relationship? (If you are part of that very small percentage of the population that has a <u>great</u> relationship, this doesn't apply to you.)

That is because they fit when they have a relationship. In this reality, almost everyone is looking to fit, looking to try to benefit, looking to win, and looking not to lose.

In this wonderful reality, you fit when you have a relationship. You benefit by people not thinking you're a loser. When you have someone to have sex with, you win. You are a winner! Now, funny enough, it is irrelevant whether you are actually having sex or not....

When you have someone to have sex with, when you have someone to copulate with, you are by definition a winner in this reality. Everybody wants to be a winner, right? Is that one of the reasons why you've striven to be with someone even when you really didn't necessarily want to be with anyone???

So there's very little honesty in this area because people want to prove that they're not losing. They want to prove that they fit with everybody else, and they want to prove that they're winning ... Great strategy. It's a major part of what keeps all of us lying to ourselves and each other about what's really going on for us.

What if you didn't have to buy that anymore? What other possibilities might open up for you? All of us? How many relationships have you chosen that were not a contribution to your life, but allowed you to end the stigma of being alone? No longer being alone, by the way, is another reason why 90% of people would rather have a bad relationship than no relationship.

How insane is that?

Whose reality are we all validating? Whose reality are we living anyway?

Who will be the first one to dare to say: *"Hey, I choose differently. I choose me."* Here's the really weird part. The people that have chosen that have oftentimes been able to finally create the relationship *that worked for them*—*even if it was different than what they were told they were supposed to choose by everybody else's point of view.*

Is that of any interest to you? If it is ... *everything that doesn't allow that to show up for you, will you destroy and uncreate that please? Right and Wrong, Good and Bad, POD and POC, All Nine, Shorts, Boys and Beyonds.*™

Everything you bought about needing to have a relationship and sex so you can fit, benefit, win, and finally not feel like a loser, will you destroy and uncreate all that please? Right and Wrong, Good and Bad, POD and POC, All Nine, Shorts, Boys and Beyonds.™ *Thank you. (Hint: you may need to run that one 30 times a day for the next 30 days. It's a very deep well.)*

Could There Be Something Even Greater Than Love?

What if instead of striving for love you were willing to have gratitude, caring and no judgment? If you were willing to choose that instead, it would take you out of all the judgments that are attached to that program of love....

What is it I just said?

Get you out of the program of LOVE? *(Blasphemy!)*

I know that for many of you, this goes against your most basic beliefs.

Love is beauty.
Love is God.
Love is what will save us.
Love is the very core of our very being.

Right?

But how many definitions of love are there? Do you realize that the word love has more definitions than almost any other word?

So when I say *I love you*, what does that mean to you? Is it kind of like this?

"I love you and only you, and I don't ever want to be with anybody else, and I don't ever think of anybody else, nor do I ever want to receive anything from anybody else, nor do I want to give anything to anybody else. You are my one and only! I love you! Oh, by the way ... I expect the same from you."

Now—is that the same as it means to me? No ...

It means something different to every one of us.

Yet, we expect that when we tell someone *I love you* that it means the same thing to him or her as it does to us! It can't! They have had a totally different life, a totally different upbringing, totally different experiences than we've had.

It's a huge source of confusion! Because we're all so busy searching for the ideal of unconditional love, we don't realize it!

What if "love" is a societal programming designed to make sure that what you know should be possible as unconditional love (love with no judgment of right, wrong, good, bad, or anything else) never shows up?

Where do you see unconditional love in the world? Where do you see someone in the world choosing it? *Except you!*

You are trying to do it all the time, and never succeeding, judging you constantly; *"Why can't I do this? Why can't I affect this change in the world? Why can't I make this occur? Why am I the only one who seems to know this is possible?"*

How do I know? Because I was one of those people.

I KNEW it should be possible. I always judged myself for all the places in which I couldn't create it. (I'm sure you've never done that though....)

You keep trying to uphold the ideal of what love is supposed to be, while seeing no one else around you choosing it. At which point, you want to come out of love and just kill them for not seeing what's possible. Cute, and not necessarily your brightest choice, my friend.

Have you been programmed to view love as the ultimate possibility? Is it? OR ARE YOU? Love is designed to get you to reach for something outside of you, and it's not actually possible to create what love is supposed to create through that venue. But it is possible through being you.

What if instead of just love you were willing to have gratitude, caring and no judgment—FOR YOU?

If you were willing to choose that instead, it would take you out of all the judgments that are attached to that program of love ... And, each of those—gratitude, caring, and no judgment—are actually possible to have and be! And they don't require you to look outside of you for something that is impossible to find. If you were willing to have them for you, they would almost magically be available for everyone else, also.

And is it possible that the combination of gratitude, caring and no judgment more closely matches the energy of what you thought you were going to get from love?

If so, you might just find that you can finally now create what you thought love was going to give you.

❧ ❧ ❧

My Friend, Do You Know That You Are Psychic?

Have you ever been in relationship? Of some kind? I will assume you have.

Let's say you were going to give your partner a call—did you know before they answered the phone when they were angry? Or when they were sad? Or when they needed you to call? Or when they needed to have a "talk"?

You knew every single time. (Whether you are willing to admit it or not.) In fact, I would wager that the reason you called them in the first place is because you knew they were in a funk or needed something from you. Don't take my word for it. Just check it out in your own life and see.

How do you know these things? *Because you're psychic! You're aware of those kinds of energies.*

You've been aware of them your entire life. Please note, when I say psychic, I'm not talking about Madame Rosinka reading your palm or Miss Chloe reading your cards. I'm talking about a person who is aware of energies. If you were willing to hone that skill, you could do all kinds of things with it.

But, for now, I'm talking about someone (YOU) that is aware of the energies around you (for example, the thoughts, feelings and emotions of those you care about).

From the moment you were conceived you've been picking up the thoughts feelings and emotions and the sexual points of view of all the people around you. Initially you were trying to figure out how to do this reality.

How does Mom do this reality?
How does Dad do this reality?
How do my siblings do this reality?
How do my relatives do this reality?
How do my friends do this reality?

You'd suck all that in and you'd become a propagation of all these people's points of view of what this reality is … hardly any of which includes you, because you weren't asking, *"What would I like as reality?"* You were asking, *"How do they do it here on this weird planet? How do I fit in here? How do I do it right? How do I do it like everyone else here? How do I win and not lose here?"*

So you're walking around doing it how everybody else does it, as though that's the only way it can be done. Part of what you were sold was this great idea of how relationships work … It's only because you're as psychic as you be, my friend. Because you could pick up on everyone else's hopes, dreams, realities and insanities.

I know, you didn't want to hear that!

But if your current relationship goes down the same old path as every other relationship has, are you aware that YOU MUST BE THE ONE that chose that path?

Isn't that kind of cool? Because if every other relationship that you've been in goes down the same path, what is the common denominator in those relationships? YOU!

Who is the only one who can choose something different? YOU!

I know, like me, you've probably been hoping to find someone—or something—that's different … someone that GETS YOU … someone that will make all of what you've decided must be true, work. But, guess what, that will only occur when you demand that you're going to choose what works for you, regardless of anyone else's point of view and regardless of whether anyone else gets you.

Choosing this reality as the basis for your reality will never work, because it doesn't include YOU. It's always about the limitation, wrongness and judgment—not about possibilities.

So, everything you've done to choose this reality over your awareness of what you would truly like to choose, will you destroy and uncreate all that please? Right and Wrong, Good and Bad, POD and POC, All Nine, Shorts, Boys and Beyonds.™ *Thank you.*

∽ ∽ ∽

You Didn't Need Those Arms and Legs Anyway, Did Ya?

Are you aware that most relationships require you to give up most of you? Here's my favorite description of it.…

You are at your house and your really cute friend drives by. They're in a really tiny car, like a Mini-Cooper. They honk their little horn and say, *"Hey! How are you doing? Come on, come on … Want to go into relationship?"* And you answer, *"Oh my God, you're like so cute, and you drive that cute little car! I'm so ready, come on let's do it!"*

And off you go. They're in the driver's seat of course, because it's their life—and you're going into relationship with them. So you go to climb into the passenger seat where you belong.

You put your feet in, and you realize the car's too small to fit your legs …. So you just cut them off and throw them out because you won't really need them anyway, because you want to go on the ride of your life, right? They just happen to be driving this tiny little car. So, you're like … OK!

Then you go to shut the door, *"I'm ready, my legs are off so I can fit just fine in the car of your life, no problem! Good, let's go!"* You go to shut the door, and you realize, *"Oh no, my shoulders and arms are too wide to fit!"* So you cut one arm off, and then you chew the other one off—and close the door with your chin—and now you're ready!

You have no arms and no legs and finally you can go on the ride of their life! In relationship with them, in the passenger seat of their little tiny car! That is so cool. Have a good time! Come on, let's go!

That's what we do in relationships, we sweet, cute beings. How does it get any better than us?

Make no mistake, I am an expert at doing this one, my friends. So I'm not telling you you're wrong for this—only that it might not be your brightest choice.

↬ ↬ ↬

Just One Little Question That Could Start Changing This….

What if—when you meet someone that you're interested in maybe starting a relationship with—you would ask this question:

Will this person be a contribution to my life and living?

Then SHUT UP and listen to what you know. You'll get the awareness of the answer before you even finish asking the question.

Does it make you light? Then it is a yes.

Heavy? No. Don't go there!!! Ask another question:

What would it take for me to meet someone that is a contribution to my life and living?

ℴ ℴ ℴ

And What Else Is Possible?

Do you know at least one person in your life that won't divorce him or herself for anyone?

What's interesting is that if you look at how other people view this person, many say, *"Oh my God, she's such a b*tch!"* Of course you don't want to be the bitch, so you make sure to divorce you from you so people don't think you are one.

But other people will see them for what they truly are: **a leader**. From my point of view, a true leader knows where they are going, does not require followers, and is willing to go where they need to go whether anyone else goes or not.

When somebody truly doesn't divorce himself or herself, they can become a leader in the world. At the very least, they can become a leader in their own life, rather than a follower.

If you have two people who are leaders in a relationship, it actually works out really well because they are both willing to allow the other person to be exactly as they are. They both desire the other person to grow, to be more, and to expand, because they are not threatened or intimidated by it. **Rather, they are inspired by it.**

What percentage of you did you divorce in order to create your current or most recent relationship? More than 100% or less? Or a LOT MORE? For most people, it's a LOT MORE. Everything you did to divorce you, will you destroy and uncreate all of that now please, and reclaim all the parts of you that you thought you had to get rid of? Right and Wrong, Good and Bad, POD and POC, All Nine, Shorts, Boys and Beyonds.™ Thank you.

What if the greatest gift to your relationship were you—willing to be as brilliantly, beautifully, amazingly, bizarrely, weirdly, intensely and joyfully different as you truly be, without divorcing any of you? Everything that doesn't allow you to choose that with ease, will you destroy and uncreate all that please? Right and Wrong, Good and Bad, POD and POC, All Nine, Shorts, Boys and Beyonds.™ Thank you.

The people who have the best relationships actually have their own lives.

They're not looking for the other person to validate them, and they're not looking for the other person to complete anything in them. They know they are complete unto themselves in their own life and living. They are also willing to have the other person as an addition to their life and living and a contribution to it—not a replacement for it.

What if you were willing to have that? Everything that doesn't allow that to show up for you, will you destroy and uncreate all of that please? Right and Wrong, Good and Bad, POD and POC, All Nine, Shorts, Boys and Beyonds.™ Thank you.

൙ ൙ ൙

Are You Willing to Try a New Way of Relating to Everyone and Everything?

There is this little thing called INTIMACY—where you are in Communion or Oneness. Where everything exists and nothing is judged. In Oneness, I can be you, you can be me.

True intimacy has five elements:

Honoring, Trust, Allowance, Vulnerability and Gratitude.

Notice that you don't see copulation in there? Surprised?

Intimacy is something that you can have with everybody, if you're willing to. It doesn't require the sex (copulation) part at all.

Strangely enough, there is one person who makes the whole difference here … If you were willing to be intimate with this one person—it would give you the choice to have it with anyone else in your life, as it worked for you and as you desired it.

By being intimate with you.

Let's have a look at the five elements:

#1 Honoring

This means being honoring of you, and honoring of your partner. To honor means to treat with regard. In all ways. Always.

As an example, have you been attracted to somebody or has someone ever been attracted to you because of the sexualness you have available? Then when you're in relationship, you decide: *"Oh my God, I can't flirt with anybody else because that would be totally dishonoring of my partner!"*

Except, what if that weren't dishonoring of your partner? What if it were part of what they loved about you in the first place? What if cutting that off was actually dishonoring of your partner? And dishonoring of you? Because you flirt, doesn't mean you're going home with someone … ever. Because you flirt means … you're flirtatious! It might mean you're a little more alive!

It might mean you're a little more fun! You might ask your partner how they feel about it before you go about eliminating some part of you that they may adore.

I know, it is a slightly different way of looking at honoring.
My question is: *Is it light for you?*

Part of this information came from a 95-year-old woman named Mary. When my friend Gary asked her if her traveling-salesman-husband, Bill, ever cheated on her when he was away, she surprised both of us with her answer. She said, "I don't know. If he needed to do that to honor himself, he would never dishonor me and our relationship by coming home and telling me about it. You young people think you need to take your dirty underwear and put it over your partner's face and demand that they love you anyway. That's crazy!"

Say what? Her response had Gary and I talking for quite a long time about what honoring really was. We realized that she had just given both of us a great gift by sharing her point of view with us. This was from a woman who was raised by her Victorian grandmother! From that day, I realized that what it means to honor someone looks a lot different than I thought it did.

Perhaps you could look at what it would mean for you to honor you and for you to honor your partner—not from the definitions you've already been given—but from what works for you, even if it's different than that.

Everything that doesn't allow you to be aware of, and actually choose, what true honoring is FOR YOU AND YOUR PARTNER, will you destroy and uncreate that please? Right and Wrong, Good and Bad, POD and POC, All Nine, Shorts, Boys and Beyonds.™

#2 Trusting

Most people think trust means blind faith. It doesn't. Many people in relationship have this idea that, *"Well, I know they were an alcoholic before being with me, but now that they're together with me, and once they see how much I love them, I trust that they will stop."* No, my dear, they're not going to stop.

What you have to trust is the person will be exactly as they were the moment you met them.

If you're going to trust that they are going to change because they love you so much, you are setting yourself up for a dismal, abysmal failure in the relationship. That's blind faith (emphasis on blind) and it doesn't work. Does that make sense?

So trust that the person you are in relationship will be themselves, warts and all, tomorrow, just as they were today. Why? Because it will make your life easier. It will make their life easier, also. It will create the possibility for a great relationship. Then if they change "for the better," it can be a pleasant surprise for both of you that makes the relationship better—not something you expect so you can finally turn them into the perfect mate.

The other aspect of trust is trusting you. To have trust in you, you have to be willing to know that you know, and to know that you will choose what's best for you.

Everything that doesn't allow that to show up for you, will you destroy and uncreate that please? Right and Wrong, Good and Bad, POD and POC, All Nine, Shorts, Boys and Beyonds.™

#3 Allowance

Allowance is where everything the other person—well anyone—chooses is just an interesting point of view. It's just a choice, and it's just an interesting point of view.

Most of us have learned to align and agree or resist and react to every point of view we are presented with. Aligning and agreeing is, in essence, judging the point of view as right, accurate and real. Resisting and reacting is judging it as something wrong and something to be avoided or to run away from at all costs.

The moment you go into judgment, you're out of allowance and out of intimacy. You can either have intimacy or judgment. Your choice.

Notice that judgment is not honoring? Nor does it invite gratitude, nor does it engender trust, nor does it allow vulnerability, nor is it allowance.

In allowance everything is an interesting point of view. No matter what you or other people choose, it is just an interesting point of view. What if all of your points of view could be just interesting points of view? Would you and your partner have more ease? More freedom? Less judgment? In fact, this is one of the keys to eliminating judgment in your life and going beyond it.

Everything that doesn't allow total allowance to become a reality for you, will you destroy and uncreate that please? Right and Wrong, Good and Bad, POD and POC, All Nine, Shorts, Boys and Beyonds.™

#4 Vulnerability

The next element of intimacy is vulnerability.

Vulnerability is like the open wound. It's where you have absolutely no barriers up to anything the other person does, to anything you do, and you don't have to prove anything about whom you are. You can just be there, being you.

Have you ever had an open sore on your body, and it's so intense that when the wind blows it's like … *whew!* That's like vulnerability. Why is that a good thing?

In this reality, what you're told is vulnerability is a bad thing. *"Oh this relationship hurt me so I'm going to put up barriers so that never happens again."* Once you put up enough of those walls and barriers—who is the one trapped behind those walls?

You are, by the barriers you erected.

So how many barriers have you erected so you wouldn't be vulnerable anymore?

Which made it so you believed that you wouldn't be hurt anymore, which instead makes it so you continually hurt you, and judge you and your partner? Will you destroy and uncreate all that please? Right and Wrong, Good and Bad, POD and POC, All Nine, Shorts, Boys, and Beyonds.™

For every single one of those barriers you erect, you have to judge whether you're doing it right or not, and whether it's working or not, and whether it is indeed keeping out the bad evil thing you wanted to keep out—which keeps you in a constant state of judgment—and takes a huge amount of energy.

If you're truly willing to be there with no barriers with someone, it creates a totally different possibility. It creates a softness in you, a receiving of everything, and it invites that possibility for them as well.

Vulnerability, in direct contrast to what you've been told, is not weakness. On the contrary, it's the place of true power and potency. Why? Because when you have no barriers and no judgments, you can have total awareness of everything because you have nothing shutting it off and total power and potency available.

Everything that doesn't allow you to have the potency that true vulnerability is for you, will you destroy and uncreate that please? Right and Wrong, Good and Bad, POD and POC, All Nine, Shorts, Boys and Beyond.™ Thank you.

#5 Gratitude

Think of someone you say you love. Get that energy for a moment. Now, instead, try having gratitude for him or her. *Is it lighter for you?*

Have you noticed you are perfectly capable of having love and judgment at the same time? In fact, you judge yourself.

You judge to see how much you love someone and how they're loving you, or not loving you, and how you're living up to it, or not living up to it....

What's the ultimate intimate love here? The ultimate intimate love is when you cut everybody else out of your life to be with just one person. That's why so many people give up their friends when they get into a relationship. How much judgment does that take? Truly, in this reality, love and judgment go hand in hand.

If you've been with somebody longer than 10 seconds, you're already in judgment of him or her. That's why the longer you're with someone the more separate you feel from them. You build walls of judgment around you and they build walls of judgment around them, and then you can't get any closer than the walls of judgment will allow.

Everything you've done to erect those walls of judgment around you that keep you from total caring, gratitude and receiving, will you destroy and uncreate it all please? Right and Wrong, Good and Bad, POD and POC, All Nine, Shorts, Boys and Beyonds.™ Thank you.

It's a huge sadness. But that's the paradigm of relationship we were handed.

What if gratitude were the new paradigm?

You can't have gratitude and judgment at the same time. You can either be grateful or have judgment: they don't co-exist. Which would you like to choose?

What is truly great about that is that someone else can have judgment of you—and you can still be grateful for him or her and even grateful for his or her judgments of you. That's pretty cool! Why? Because it gives you, you—and there is no need to ever separate from anyone ever again. Not even you. It creates the possibility of being grateful for everything your partner chooses.

Everything that doesn't allow that to become a reality for you, will you destroy and uncreate that please? Right and Wrong, Good and Bad, POD and POC, All Nine, Shorts, Boys and Beyonds.™ Thank you.

ഗ ഗ ഗ

Love: Part Deux
Are You Willing to Choose Intimacy with Yourself?

Now my friend, if you had these five elements in your relationships—with men, women, friends, parents, children—would that open up new possibilities for you?

If you look at what you actually wanted when you spoke of **love**, does it seem more like gratitude, honoring, trust, allowance and vulnerability? And what if we add caring, nurturing and kindness and no judgment to that?

Truth? Is that what you desire for others?

Is it what you desire for you?

Would you be willing to choose intimacy with yourself? Love or not?

Please know, just because you are intimate with you, it doesn't mean you wouldn't choose to have someone else in your life. It doesn't mean that you have to go off and be alone....

On the contrary, what it does mean is that instead of choosing some person who wants to diminish and limit you, you will actually choose someone who is a contribution to your life. You will no longer believe that you need someone, and the rightness of their judgments, to make you whole and complete.

Everything that doesn't allow that to show up for you to choose that with total ease, will you destroy and uncreate all that please? Right and Wrong, Good and Bad, POD and POC, All Nine, Shorts, Boys and Beyonds.™ Thank you.

My point of view is: if you want to have a relationship, you should have a great and phenomenal one!

From my point of view, why settle for someone who is going to fulfill your need to fit with the rest of the limited world other people find so valuable? Relationship is awesome so long as it is a contribution to your life.

Everything that doesn't allow you to perceive, know, be and receive that as a possibility—and how to create it—will you let that go now and destroy and uncreate all that please? Right and Wrong, Good and Bad, POD and POC, All Nine, Shorts, Boys and Beyonds.™ Thank you.

Now you know that is a possibility.

You just have to say: *"OK, I will choose that."*

Everything that doesn't allow that to show up, will you destroy and uncreate all that now please? Right and Wrong, Good and Bad, POD and POC, All Nine, Shorts, Boys and Beyonds.™ Thank you.

---------------- TOOL ----------------

Destroying Your Relationships Every Day

Here's another weird tool. One that can change the way your life flows.

We're all stuck in each other.

We have shared expectations, projections, illusions,
delusions, memories, roles that we be with each other.
We're stuck in them.

How might it be possible to be with each other without all that baggage?

Would your way of being with your partner, mother,
father, child, colleague be any different?

**What if you started every morning by uncreating and
destroying all your relationships?** In total gratitude for
everything that has been—and for what is to come? Why? So
you can be constantly creating and generating with the people
you are in relationship with, rather than weighing yourself
down by carrying around the past.

Also, if you look at my alternative meaning of relationship—in essence
meaning "not Oneness,"—you might think of it as destroying all the places
you haven't been able to be in allowance, oneness and no judgment of those
you are in relationship with.

How? It's easy. Like this.

*I now uncreate and destroy my relationship to [my partner's name]. Right and Wrong,
Good and Bad, POD and POC, All Nine, Shorts, Boys and Beyonds.*™ *Thank you.*

*I now uncreate and destroy my relationship to my family. Right and
Wrong, Good and Bad, POD and POC, All Nine, Shorts, Boys and
Beyonds.*™ *Thank you.*

*I now uncreate and destroy my relationship to my job, work and everyone
I work with. Right and Wrong, Good and Bad, POD and POC, All
Nine, Shorts, Boys and Beyonds.*™ *Thank you.*

*I now uncreate and destroy my relationship to me. Right and Wrong,
Good and Bad, POD and POC, All Nine, Shorts, Boys and Beyonds.*™
Thank you.

*(If you're one of those people who likes words, you can add the
following words to the processes above. If you're not, just ignore this part.)*

*I now uncreate and destroy my relationship to [my partner's name], and
every projection, expectation, separation, judgment and rejection either
of us has about each other or our relationship, from the past, present or
future. Right and Wrong, Good and Bad, POD and POC, All Nine,
Shorts, Boys and Beyonds.*™

Now—start a truly NEW DAY.

**With less past baggage and more future
possibilities.**

---- TOOL ----

A New Paradigm for Change

Here's a quick 5-STEP GUIDE TO CHANGING ANYTHING IN YOUR LIFE! For example, a relationship. It could be to anyone—your lover, your boss, your partner ... the Universe.

1. First—make a demand.
As in, "Hey, this is going to change and something else is going to show up!"

Have you ever noticed that when you're in relationship and you know it needs to change, but you're not willing to demand that it change, but you know it needs to, but you're not really willing to demand it, but you know it needs to, and finally when you get to the point where, *"Enough knowing it needs to, this is going to change, I don't care if I die, I don't care if they die, it doesn't matter, I don't care if the world ends, this is changing now!"*

Remember how quickly it changes? **That is a demand.**

2. Next—ask a question.
Every question you ask opens up a completely different possibility and a new potential.

You're making this demand, and then you ask—*Hey, what's it going to take for this to show up differently?* All of a sudden this doorway opens up you never saw before, you stick your head in the doorway, and there're all these different paths you can take.

You couldn't see them until you made the demand and asked the question.

3. Third—*wave the magic wand.*

Ask to destroy and uncreate and let go of everything you've created or
bought that doesn't allow that to show up as soon as possible. Then run
the clearing statement: *Right and Wrong, Good and Bad, POD and POC, All
Nine, Shorts, Boys and Beyonds.*™
(Or just POC and POD all that!')

4. Now—*CHOOSE (and ACT)!*

Your choice determines the potentials that will occur.
In other words, you've got the demand, the question, and the letting go of
the limitation—and it's the choice that actually creates a different potential
for the future. You have to choose (and ACT)!

This is a reality where doing is often required to create things. In other
words, you can't just sit on your butt and expect change to occur! We have
been sold a huge unkindness by the people that believe that you JUST ask
and receive. In this reality, you still have to DO TOO! Please don't limit
what can show up for you by refusing to act when it's necessary. Asking is
one very important step in the process—it's not the end.

If you want to know what actions to take, simply ask this question every
day, *"What can I do today that will allow this to show up right away?"*

One of your greatest capacities as a being is the capacity to choose. What
most of us like to do is have one choice that's going to rule the rest of our
lives. (I like to call that the *Lord of the Rings* choice: "One Choice to Rule
Them All!"). We think we should choose only the good (right) things and
not the bad (wrong) things. But that takes A LOT of judgment—of us.

What if there were no judgment of, *"Oh, this is a good thing,"* or *"Oh, this is a
bad thing?"* What if it were just, *"Wow, I made that choice."* And if it works out
well, choose more of that. If it doesn't work out well, what if you could
just choose again?

That's another aspect of the magic of you—the
capacity to always choose again.

Now.

♋ ♋ ♋ ♋ ♋ ♋

And now.

♋ ♋ ♋ ♋ ♋ ♋

And now.
With this, as with all things, if you see something you desire, would you be
willing to start moving in the direction of it showing up today? Better yet,
NOW. Start demanding change, ask questions, be willing to let go of your
limitations, CHOOSE something different, and then ACT!

5. Finally—RECEIVE everything.
For this to work, for things to change, you have to be willing to receive
everything that shows up, with no judgment or exclusion. Trust the
Universe.

Please know, you don't control when something shows up, or exactly what
it looks like. The Universe does. The Universe is aware of INFINITE
possibilities—
possibilities that go way, way, WAY beyond every
fantasy you may have of what the perfect—for
example, relationship—should look like.

Because you are not alone in the world, the Universe has to re-arrange a lot
of people's universes in order to create a major outward shift in the world.
You may ask today and receive it in 10 years—or 10 seconds from now.
So if it doesn't show up tomorrow—you are NOT wrong, my friend.

It will occur. You have started!
Right now … reading this….
And please know—it will probably look completely different than you've
ever imagined.

Sex

ualness

Please Know....

One of the most seductive
things in the world
is when someone looks at you
with no judgment.

When that happens
your whole being goes:
"Please don't leave.
Please don't go. Stay, please."

Are you willing to be that?

For you?

— Chapter 7 —
Let's Talk About Sex, Baby....

My dear beautiful friends, part of the reason we judge our bodies and feel disconnected and separate from them is because we haven't ever really received much kindness or caring with them.

It is one of life's greatest travesties. It's one of the great sadnesses of this reality. We don't have a place or space where our bodies are just nurtured and cared for.

We often cut off sex because of the experiences we have had that were dishonoring and unkind and not the beauty and sensation and joy and fun and lightness and possibility that two bodies getting together can—and could—be. And in our desire to cut off sex, we cut off that energy of receiving and gifting that could occur between *all of our bodies*.

Would you consider instead embracing your **sexualness?**

Sexualness includes: **healing, caring, nurturing, joyful, generative, creative, expansive and orgasmic energy.**

Everything that doesn't allow that wonderful energy of sexualness to become a reality for you, will you destroy and uncreate all that, please? Right and Wrong, Good and Bad, POD and POC, All Nine, Shorts, Boys and Beyonds.™

It is one of those energies we've killed in our lives—the energy of sexualness. Please note, I'm not saying sexuality. I'm saying sexualness. **It has a totally different meaning.**

I'm going to write it one more time since it's such a different concept: Sexualness is healing, caring, nurturing, expansive, joyful, generative, creative and orgasmic. *That's the energy of sexualness.*

And sexualness is not about putting the body parts together. It's about the being and the energy our bodies actually have. It's kind of like puppies cuddling together. And couldn't we all use a bit more puppy-like cuddling? I think so! When your body is functioning from sexualness it will be turned on … turned on like the power switch is on, turned on in the way of *"whoo-hoo, we're alive!"*

Yes, copulation (sex) would be really fun from that place, but it's truly not necessary—and sexualness is about so much more than just that.

It is the **energy of living** that we have been taught to turn off since we were little. I say again, it is NOT copulation. Copulation is putting the body parts together. And that should always be a choice.

Once again....

Sexualness:

Healing, caring, nurturing, expansive, joyful, generative, creative and orgasmic energy of being.

Copulation:

Putting the body parts together.

This is the beginning of a different paradigm for being with your body, and in your world, that actually allows you to receive totally, gift openly and change the harshness and unkindness that this reality has become.

Just check if it is light for you....

And let me give you two examples. The first one I've used previously.

ഇ ഇ ഇ

The Hug

Imagine having a nurturing hug from someone—one of those hugs where you just melt into them and they melt into you—and you feel like your universe and theirs could just go on and on and on and on....

Notice there's no copulation in it, but there is total sexualness present. (If you look again at the aspects of sexualness, you'll see that they are all encompassed by that nurturing, world-expanding hug.) Notice, also, that because there's no sexuality in it, because you don't have to judge what you won't receive and you don't have to prove anything, there's also no weirdness.

After all, it's just a hug.

My question is: *What if copulation could be as nurturing and spacious as—and even more fun than—a great hug?*

ഇ ഇ ഇ

Being a Doctor of Chiropractic

When I want to chiropractic college, I was told to cut off all of my sexual energy in order not to be sued. In other words, I was told not to be the energy of sexualness.

I was supposed to put my hands on people to heal them and change things for their bodies and their lives, while cutting off the very energy of healing, nurturing and caring energy that allows me to do it.

For me that is insane.

Just look at it—did you go into judgment there, even for just a second? That comes from never being given the awareness that there is a difference between sexualness and sexuality! There is—and it is a fundamental difference.

Looking back, I think that what "they" wanted me to eliminate was the sexuality, that weird, forceful, judgmental, unkind energy that some people put on others about wanting to copulate with them. But "they" never made any distinction, probably because "they" didn't know there was a difference. So I was left believing that I was somehow supposed to cut off EVERYTHING, including me, which is what sexualness is. (Because sexualness includes you, as well as everyone else. Sexualness includes. Sexuality excludes.)

That's why I am delineating this area for you: so you don't have to cut off your sexualness any longer, just because you are someone who doesn't want to impose on others that weird, judgmental, bizarrely unkind, un-nurturing energy of sexuality which may not be a part of you at all.

AGAIN—THERE IS A DIFFERENCE! (I know this is really weird for some of you.)

Sexuality: always a judgment, and often a proving of "see how sexual I am," with no receiving, and often invoking a weird feeling of inadequacy and wrongness.

Sexualness: the non-judgmental, healing, caring, nurturing, joyful, generative, expansive, creative and orgasmic energy that can not only heal bodies and lives, but also change the face of the world.

Which would you prefer to choose? Have you, too, been taught to cut off the energy of sexualness from a very young age? Most of us have, unfortunately.

So everything you've done to turn off that sexualness, to judge it, to have it judged in you, as though you were a bad person if you had it, or as though you were going to turn out to be a bad person, a slut or something, if you were actually that sexual, will you destroy and uncreate it please? Right and Wrong, Good and Bad, POD and POC, All Nine, Shorts, Boys and Beyonds.™

And will you please now allow the healing, caring, nurturing , joyful, creative, generative and orgasmic energy you truly be to show up in totality, with ease? Right and Wrong, Good and Bad, POD and POC, All Nine, Shorts, Boys and Beyonds.™ Thank you.

⬦ ⬦ ⬦

Orgasmic Gratitude? (Orgasmitude???)

Imagine if you were to be totally grateful for you? For everything you be, every part of you.

What would that be like? Would that be healing? Would it be caring and nurturing? Yes, because if you're grateful for you, you're not in judgment of you since you can't have gratitude and judgment at the same time. Would it be joyful? Yes, because true joy is a sense of peace. And you can truly have peace when you are beyond judging you. Would it be nurturing? Yes, because not judging you is one of the most nurturing things you can do for yourself.

Would it be generative? Would it be creative? In other words can you bring different things into existence and into reality because of it? Yep.

And would it be orgasmic?

Having gratitude for you and total sexualness go hand and hand. You can't have gratitude and judgment at the same time, and you can't have sexualness and judgment at the same time either. Judgment always eliminates sexualness.

A choice for being sexualness rises above the limitation imposed by judgment. (You may want to flip back and read the elements of sexualness one more time if this isn't making sense.)

Truly, if you got how wonderful it could be to have total sexualness and total gratitude together, why would you ever choose anything else? Why would you ever choose to judge you again? And you're not choosing that right now for what reason?

All the projections, expectations, separations, judgments and rejections you have been imposing on you that create the impelled need of sexuality and the destruction of sexualness, will you destroy and uncreate all that please? Right and Wrong, Good and Bad, POD and POC, All Nine, Shorts, Boys and Beyonds.™ *Thank you.*

Everything that does not allow you to choose to have total sexualness and total gratitude for you and your body (and the joy that would bring) will you destroy and uncreate all of that please? Right and Wrong, Good and Bad, POD and POC, All Nine, Shorts, Boys and Beyonds.™ *Thank you.*

∽ ∽ ∽

Being an Invitation

When you're being sexualness, you're an invitation for everybody. You're the healing possibility and the caring possibility that they don't have in their lives. You become the nurturing they don't have in their lives, the joyfulness that they don't have in their lives, the generative capacity they don't have in their lives, the creative capacity—the expansiveness, and the orgasmic possibility of living. And you don't have to copulate with them—ever—to be that.

Sexuality on the other hand is, *"Our interaction is only about what I get from you through copulation. That's the means, the end and the goal. I want to give it to you, and I want to copulate with you. And if we don't copulate, then we have no business interacting with each other."*

So would you consider the possibility that having the energy of sexualness could actually be a joyful expression of life and living? Everything that doesn't allow that to show up for you, will you destroy and uncreate that please? Right and Wrong, Good and Bad, POD and POC, All Nine, Shorts, Boys and Beyonds.™ Thank you.

Would you be willing to embrace more of the sexualness that you truly are that you didn't know existed until you read it a few minutes ago? Would you be willing to destroy and uncreate all of your preconceived conditions of sexuality and judgment that really aren't working for you? Right and Wrong, Good and Bad, POD and POC, All Nine, Shorts, Boys and Beyonds.™ Thank you.

Please understand, I am not trying to impose a point of view on you. Really. What I am attempting to do is invite you to a completely different possibility for living. As always, please don't try to buy anything here that doesn't work for you. But at least try it on.

If someone had given me these distinctions and tools 11 years ago, I might have been in a happier place.

Part of my depression was that what I saw in the world and what other people saw as reality were just so different than what I KNEW should be available. Having almost no one else see as valuable what I considered the value and joy and reasons for living—kindness, caring, healing, nurturing, joyful, generative, expansive, creative and orgasmic energies, and no judgment —which was everything I wanted to have in the world—made me doubt whether it would or could ever show up. And if those things couldn't show up, from my point of view, it wasn't worth living.

Now they do. And life is worth living!

Orgasmic and Un-Stoppable?

If you had that energy of sexualness, would you be stoppable or unstoppable?

Unstoppable.

Having that, would you choose to bend and waiver according to other people's judgments? Why would you choose to bend according to the heaviness of their judgments when there's so much fun to be had? You'd be unjudgable because their judgments would no longer have any effect on you. Therefore, you'd be unstoppable, and unlimitable and no one could control you.

Oh yeah, you'd also be really joyful, and a lot kinder—to you and everyone else—and you'd have a lot more energy. How many people in your life would be totally intimidated by that? Almost all of them—except for the ones that are willing to be that orgasmic too.

Would you be willing to have—and be—more fun?
Would you be willing to be unstoppable?
Would you be willing to be more orgasmic? (Because orgasm is the energy that creates life.)

Everything that doesn't allow that to show up, will you destroy and uncreate all that now please? Right and Wrong, Good and Bad, POD and POC, All Nine, Shorts, Boys and Beyonds.™ Thank you.

By the way, it doesn't require that you copulate—ever.

What if you could choose to have that wonderful orgasmic energy whenever you desired it?

What Would It Take to Actually Have Orgasmic Living?

"Orgasmic what?!?!?" you say.

Orgasmic living! That's where you choose your life and the experiences you have because they are fun, joyful, intensely wonderful and expansive.

What would that take?

One of the things it requires is choice on your part. You have to be willing to have orgasmic living as something valuable—rather than something you try to avoid at all costs so you can be normal, average, real and the same as everyone else.

You have to be willing to have it as a contribution to your life, rather than seeing it as a bad thing.

Would you be willing to have a totally different point of view?

Will you do me (and you) a favor, please? Will you please let go of the idea that you have to have sex (copulation) in order to have orgasm? Instead, will you please let it be an energy of joyous possibility and generation flowing through your **entire** life and living?

Continuously.

(Just because you take the necessity of copulation out of orgasm, please don't take the orgasm out of copulation!)

What do I mean? Well, have you ever had a bite of food that tasted so deliciously yummy, so tasty, with so many levels of flavor coursing through it, that you could feel it through every cell of your whole body? Is that orgasmic? Yes! (By the way, if you haven't, it's time!)

Have you ever gone downhill skiing so fast that you were laughing so hard you thought you were going to pee your pants? Was it orgasmic? *Yes!*

Have you ever sat on the beach, or in the mountains, with the sun caressing your skin, feeling so very blessed to be alive that you felt at one with everything? Was it orgasmic? *Yes!*

Have you ever taken a bath where from the moment you climbed into the steaming water your body was all abuzz and aglow with the intensity and sensations of it? Orgasmic? *Yes again!*

All of those are the experiences of orgasmic living. They are just a tiny portion of the infinite possibilities that are available. Notice that not one of them involved copulation? *Weird, eh?* What would it be like if it were more valuable to you to have more of your life show up like that? Wouldn't that be a lot more fun?

So what are you waiting for? You're being given the tools. Create the change that allows that to show up! You may just barely open the door for that to happen today, but if you don't ever open it, it will stay shut forever. If you open it now, it may just stay open forever. Your choice.

Orgasmic living—or being normal, average, real and the same as every other boring person you've ever known. Which would you like to choose? The funny part is … it's really just a choice.

And what, exactly, are those tools that you have? Let me give you a quick review here:

1. DEMAND: Make a demand that the way things were showing up is changing now and something different is going to show up.

2. ASK: Ask, "What's it going to take for this to show up?" and "What can I change, choose, and contribute and receive that will allow this to show up?"

3. POD and POC: Ask to destroy and uncreate and let go of everything that doesn't allow that to show up as soon as possible. And then run that clearing statement: *Right and Wrong, Good and Bad, POD and POC, All Nine, Shorts, Boys and Beyonds.*™

4. CHOOSE and ACT: Your choice determines the potentials that will occur. In other words, you've got the demand, the question, letting go of the limitation—and it's the choice—and action—that actually creates a different potential for the future. You have to choose!

5. RECEIVE *everything*. Please know, you don't control when something shows up, or exactly how it looks. The Universe does. For this to work, for things to change, you have to be willing to receive everything that shows up, with no judgment or exclusion.

There you have it: a recap of the short form for changing anything.

Too weird? That's OK. You really didn't want that change anyway, did you?

Especially not this sexualness thing....
Who would want to be orgasmic anyway? Really?

Orgasmic Body: How to Have More Energy at Any Time, with Total Ease

Start by remembering the last time you had an orgasm. (Even if it was 150 years ago....)

Now, bring that orgasmic energy up from the Earth.

The Earth has a huge amount of it—it's like a big pulsing hot orgasm....

How else could it have a molten core that takes hundreds of millions—or billions—of years to go cold?

OK, bring the energy of orgasm from the earth through your feet, into your ankles, through your knees, through your hips, through your belly, through your solar plexus and chest, through your arms, through your neck and out the top of your head.

More. ∽ ∽ ∽ ∽ ∽ ∽ ∽ More! ∽ ∽ ∽ ∽ ∽ ∽ ∽ ∽
More!!! ∽ ∽ ∽ ∽ ∽ ∽ ∽ More!!!!

How does your body feel now?
Oh, by the way, if your sweet body wants to move in a particular way at this point, please ... let it!

If you started every day (and every night) this way....

That would not be good for you. At all.

(That was a joke, if you didn't catch that.)

Beyond Your

Family

(Now is that really allowed?)

It's Your Choice, NOT Your Upbringing That Creates Your Reality....

What have you chosen, just because you could, that made no sense to anyone, that is an indication to you of how different you are?

Have you perhaps experienced unkindness or abuse
and have somehow chosen to be a kind person?

Or did you grow up with little money and have chosen to change it?
Or, did you grow up with people who judged constantly, but you have chosen to go beyond the need to judge?

Will you please acknowledge that you have created
a different reality than just what you were handed
as a child?

Will you please acknowledge just how amazingly potent YOU are?

And will you acknowledge that

IT IS YOUR CHOICE, NOT YOUR UPBRINGING, THAT
CREATES YOUR LIFE AND LIVING.

— Chapter 8 —
What If You Chose
Your Parents?

Imagine this ... You are this beautiful blinking spark of being in the Universe. In the middle of doing your third somersault on a soft bubbly cloud, you choose to take on a body for a while ... Just for fun—and maybe as a step on your way to consciousness.

Anyhow, you find these two people and smash them together. Bam!

There you be! There your body is!

It is kind of a vital piece of information that we are not given....

You choose your parents, you potent little baby!

Just check it out ... Does it make you feel lighter?

Get this—when you embody, you don't just get a body, you get this whole reality! It is almost like you are watching one of those late night infomercials, and this particular one is selling lifetimes here on planet Earth.

You're watching it up there as a sparkly little being, on your little cloud, and you are going, *"Oh dude really, I could go to Earth? Wow!"*

From the CloudTV you hear: *"Yes, and if you act now you don't just get a body, you'll get every limitation this reality has to offer. You'll get to fight your way out of limited reality at every moment! You'll have it impinge upon you! You'll have it try to suffocate you! You'll have all kinds of people around you who don't want to know there's anything else available! You'll have something to fight for every moment of your life until you die to prove you were a success! But only if you act now! Operators standing by."*

And you think, *"Okay, I will do that! That sounds like an adventure."*

This is why I say: We are cute, just not very bright.

❦ ❦ ❦

Growing Up in the Ghetto

If you think your choice of parents and childhood was interesting, let me share mine with you for a moment. From the time I was two until age nine, I grew up in the ghetto. I was the only white kid for 8 square miles. I was the only white kid I knew at my school. That's an interesting choice for a child—in this case me—to make.

Luckily, though most of the people in the ghetto have a lot of hatred in their universes, many of the young children I knew hadn't learned yet to judge— and hate—based on color—yet. Sure, almost all of the older people I knew there were filled with it, but one has a way of learning to survive.

I had some really wonderful friends in the ghetto—all of whom had different-colored skin than I did. I didn't realize we were different until I was about eight years old. That's when someone first picked a fight with me for being a different color. Looking back on that is what made me realize that kids are taught to judge. It's not something we come in with.

The ghetto is really the crowning achievement of this reality. Everybody learns to hate first and ask questions later—if ever. It's that hate that permeates everything and creates the lack of hope which keeps people in this cycle and doesn't ever allow anything to change. It's that alignment and agreement and resistance and reaction to the rightness or wrongness of the points of view there that keeps everything stuck. Talk about the ultimate multi-level marketing program of crap! There's no allowance in the ghetto.

At the same time, I had wealthy grandparents and a father who was well off. So I would go visit my father or grandparents every other weekend. Then I would come back to the ghetto.

My grandmother would take off all the "nice" clothes that I had worn during the weekend with her, and then put my crappy clothes on me again because every time I went back to the house in the ghetto, the people my mom and I lived with would steal all my nice clothes—and everything else that was worth stealing. Oh, the joy!

It must have been a sight to see … My grandmother would drive up in her brand new Lincoln Continental® and drop me off in front of one of these ghetto houses, undress me outside the car, and take off my clothes and put my crummy clothes back on … It was like "Ritchie Rich meets Tito Puente."

My Dad and grandmother had the point of view that, *"We are white. We are rich. We are superior."* My point of view was, *"Try living my life. People hate me for being white here. People hate me for the thought that I have money—even though I don't!"*

So I lived in this bizarre conflictual universe. A conflictual universe is where you have one universe that's one thing and then another universe that's totally different, and you can't make them congruent. There's just no way. So you function in this conflictual universe, where you don't ever really have a clue of what's actually true … That was part of my reality growing up. Interesting choice, eh? And by the way, how much of your childhood (and your current reality) feels like a conflictual universe to you?

Everything that creates your childhood and your reality as a conflictual universe, will you destroy and uncreate it all please? Right and Wrong, Good and Bad, POD and POC, All Nine, Shorts, Boys and Beyonds.™ Thank you.

∽ ∽ ∽

I Knew. So Did You.

What I realized is that I came to give my parents the awareness that they didn't have to live in judgment. Did I succeed? No.

I used to try to see why or how I could have that much hate, anger, and vitriol directed at me on a constant basis while living in the ghetto, and still just want to give those very people a hug, and say to them, *"You don't have to be that way. Come on, let's hug."*

I wanted to figure out why and how I could be that way, because, if there were a reason I could come up with, then I could show other people how to be it, and show other people how to have it, too.

Do you suppose any of that could be true for you? Have you ever just wanted to show people that they have other choices? Have you ever wanted to just hug them and let them know that it could all be different—and a lot easier?

But, unfortunately, you can't show other people how to be it or have it.

It's a choice.

A choice that is beyond any reason and justification. Beyond everything that is cognitive.

When you choose something, no one can ever take it away.

And you always have a choice. Always.

Did You Come to Your Parents to Gift Them Something That They Refused to Receive?

What if you came to give your parents something—some gift or awareness? Maybe you came to show them that they were loved, or that they could have a greater life, or that they didn't have to suffer, or that they didn't have to judge, or that anger and sadness was not their only choice.

For most of us, because they refused to receive it, we decided we were failures. You know what? It's not that you failed—they just didn't want it. Did you hear me, my beautiful friend? **It's not that you failed. They just couldn't or wouldn't receive it—or you.**

And it's not your fault. In any way. Really. Truth. Promise.

It's not their fault, either. They just had their fixed points of view already in place. It is not that they are bad and wrong, it was just what they were willing to choose. They were doing the best they could with the tools that they had. Some of them had such woefully inadequate tools....
We are so cute (and so not bright).

What do we then do to try to change it? It seems like one thing we most often do is take the parent that loves us the least and create a relationship with someone that is just like that.

Apparently, we figure that if we can change that person, then we can finally heal what we couldn't heal in the parent who didn't love us as much as we hoped for. Then finally we might be able to come out of the judgment that we are a failure. We think finally we might be able to come out of judgment of us, because we are sure that this failure of ours must be the source of the wrongness of us that we've perceived our whole life.

Wow!

What if none of that were true? What if it wasn't your mission to heal your parents? What if there is absolutely NOTHING wrong with you? Or them? What if that nagging feeling of wrongness were from something else entirely?

If this applies to you, at what age did you decide you were a failure?

Two … four … six? Second day after birth? Second month after conception?

At whatever age you decided you were a failure because your parents refused to see the gift that you are, would you be willing to give all that up now and destroy and uncreate it and claim, own and acknowledge that you are the gift you came to be (even if you don't know what that is)? Right and Wrong, Good and Bad, POD and POC, All Nine, Shorts, Boys and Beyonds.™ Thank you.

ℝℝℝ

"You're Not ANY Better Than Us, Dear."

How much of your life have you created in order to validate your family's points of view about what's possible and what's not possible?

That's pretty much the point of view that's pervasive in the world: you cannot go and be any different—especially not greater than—your family was. You can be a little bit less than, but you cannot be greater than. You can't be freer of judgment. You can't make more money. You can't enjoy your life more than your family did, because they're the ones who taught you how to get by in this reality.

Or you spend your whole life fighting and resisting any point of view your family has—proving over and over again that you are just like them, just on the other side of the coin of their reality.

How much of your life have you spent being your Dad, while resisting being your Dad, while being your Dad, while resisting being your Dad?

How much of your life have you spent being your Mom, while resisting being your Mom, while being your Mom, while resisting being your Mom?

Everything that holds all that in place, will you let all of that go now, and destroy and uncreate it all please? Right and Wrong, Good and Bad, POD and POC, All Nine, Shorts, Boys and Beyonds.™ Thank you.

If you chose your parents, do you suppose you would be willing to look and see what gift you have received by picking these two people?

Ask this question: "What gift have I received by choosing these people as my parents?"

Everything that doesn't allow you to see the gift(s) you have received by picking the parents you picked, will you let all that go now please? Right and Wrong, Good and Bad, POD and POC, All Nine, Shorts, Boys and Beyonds.™ Thank you.

As a reminder: "What have you chosen, just because you could, that made no sense to anyone else, that is an indication to you of how different you are?"

Will you please acknowledge that you have created a different reality than just what you were handed as a child?

Will you please acknowledge just how amazingly potent YOU are?
And will you NOW acknowledge that it is YOUR CHOICE, NOT YOUR UPBRINGING, that determines your life and living?

And everything that doesn't allow that to show up for you now, will you please destroy and uncreate all that? Right and Wrong, Good and Bad, POD and POC, All Nine, Shorts, Boys and Beyonds.™ Thank you.

What would you now like to choose as your life?

The Path to Consciousness

You want to have a different world? Come out of judgment of you!

When you stop judging you, and stop judging everybody else, you become the difference and change that you've desired, and maybe even asked for, your entire life.

You be you. When you create and generate a living that is joyful for you, you are the change on the planet, and you are the gift that heals the planet. If you've ever been looking for a **"path to consciousness,"** this is it. And I don't mean my book or Access Consciousness. I mean you, being you.

It's not about going and doing some impossible task with some impossible dream in some impossible place where you don't even know what it is and you don't have the tools for.

It's not about living in a cave and meditating your whole life. It's not about forsaking this reality and all the yummy, fun stuff you can do and have and be here.

It is about living with ease, honoring yourself and others, creating your life with **everything** you would like to have in it—all with a sense of ease, joy and glory*.

THAT is what it's about.

You have the tools. You are the tools.

Now is the time, my beautiful friends.

glory: "exuberant expression and abundance"

Everything Is

Choice

— EXTRA NOTE TO READER, FROM 2012 —

I sit, rather pensive, in anticipation of re-writing this chapter of Being You, Changing the World. In order to re-write this chapter, I have to revisit a subject that I thought I had long left behind me. And in so doing, I am confronted with just how different my point of view of the world is than most of the people I call my brothers and sisters on this planet. (You.)

Previously, to me, this chapter was one chapter in a large book of possibilities. Having lived through what I will describe to you changed my entire life—literally.

But having to revisit the subject from the perspective of telling what occurred and what I learned from it in order to truly describe what might be possible for you, the readers, has opened my eyes yet again.

Let me tell you a bit more before diving into the subject at hand.

Literally two days before the Swedish version of the Being You manuscript was to be typeset, the publisher called to ask if we could remove this chapter from the book. To say I was startled is a bit of an understatement. You see, I have received literally hundreds of emails from people telling me that this one chapter (in its previous iteration) had given them a perspective that quite literally saved their lives.

My response to my very kind publisher was: "No." But in listening to her express to me her reasons for wanting to remove the chapter, I realize that in the initial Being You manuscript, I did not give enough information to you, the reader. I also realized that my reason for writing this chapter in the first place was to give people a different perspective. That it did.

But yet, more information was actually required. So, I offered to re-write the chapter to make it the chapter I wanted it to be when I wrote the book but wasn't able to write.

Yes, I change too.

I've realized that many times in our lives, when we live through an event, we often take for granted that other people will get the perspectives we have come away with as a result of that event—even though their life experience has been quite different than ours. We just seem to assume that others see the world as we do in some very fundamental ways.

You would think that, because I do what I do for a living, I would know that like the back of my hand. On one hand, I do. And on another, I have just been given a huge gift of awareness—hopefully one that will more effectively explain the potentially-controversial subjects in this chapter.

Also, this one chapter, if taken out of context of the entire book could seem harsh to people. That was not exactly the effect I was looking for.

So, what you see before you is a somewhat different chapter then you otherwise would have read if my Swedish publisher had not been looking out for you, and in the process, looking out for all of us.

Also, in the new English version, this chapter will change as of late 2012. If you want to see what the previous version said, feel free to look for a secondhand copy somewhere....

Consider this your invitation to have a totally different awareness about a few very controversial subjects that I have come to have a very different perspective about.

Okay, beautiful brothers and sisters of this beautiful planet we are lucky enough to call home, here it goes....

Understanding versus Awareness

"Do you understand?"

How many times in your life have you heard that question?

Or asked it?

Please take a moment to look at this.

Are you trying to live your life from a cognitive point of view?
Are you trying to understand how it works to get it right?
Most of us are.

Here's another possibility for you to consider. It doesn't work!

We start by having the point of view that "I think. Therefore I am."
From that, we conclude that choice is cognitive.
But it's not.

We've chosen lots of things that weren't cognitive.

And we think that understanding is awareness, but it's not.

Awareness often times has no "understanding" to it because it has no point
of view to it. It just is.

Understanding is inferior to awareness.

Understanding is a function of your mind.

Awareness is a function of you, the being.

Trying to live our lives from a cognitive point of view is one of the greatest limitations we have.

And please, don't try to get this cognitively....

Just ask. Is it light or heavy?

For you.

— Chapter 9 —

If Death Were a Choice Instead of a Wrongness, Could You Then Fully Live?

Would you be willing to dive into the deep end with me for a moment? Please?

Now, this may truly go against everything you believe in....

Okay, consider yourself warned! Hold on. And remember:

Everything is the opposite of what it appears to be,
nothing is the opposite of what it appears to be.

Everything is the opposite of what it appears to be,
nothing is the opposite of what it appears to be.

Everything is the opposite of what it appears to be,
nothing is the opposite of what it appears to be.

Everything is the opposite of what it appears to be,
nothing is the opposite of what it appears to be.

Everything is the opposite of what it appears to be,
nothing is the opposite of what it appears to be.

Do you realize that death and change are made completely wrong in this reality? Death is perceived as one of the worst things that can possibly happen to you. Incidentally, so is change. How much question is there in that point of view? None. And when you don't ask a question, you cut off your awareness—of any other perspective that might be possible.

So I wonder what could show up if we didn't make death or pain or change wrong and instead began to wonder what is actually going on here? If everything is choice, I wonder how this got created? Or for what reason? Do you see how just asking those small questions can open up a totally different possibility? They take you out of conclusion, where no other possibilities exist, and allow the doors to other possibilities to open.

Take something as horrific as 9/11. If you take the conclusion, "This is so horrible" out of it, what awareness might be there? What possibilities might be there that you haven't yet considered? The possibilities are there in almost any situation, but in order to see them, you have to be willing to look for them and ask them to show up. How do you do that? By asking questions! (Oh, that again.)

What if all those other possibilities were kind of like scared little children?

What do I mean by that?

In the world of trying to come to conclusion about everything, which we currently live in, these possibilities have been so forgotten and abandoned and told they have no value for so long, that they are now hiding. They aren't willing to come out and play anymore—unless you search for them and let them know you're willing for them to be present in your life. You do that by asking a question and then being willing to be open to a totally different possibility. This part is so important. In order for a new perspective or awareness or possibility to come into your world, YOU have to be willing to let it. Yes, YOU.

Let's give it a shot. Let's go to the event called 9/11 and look from a place of "What else is possible?" and maybe even ask some questions.

As a start, isn't it interesting that two buildings that would normally hold nearly 50,000 people, had only 3,000 die that day? In any other situation that could be considered amazing at the very least. Some would call it a miracle. What if the fact that "only" 3,000 people died that day instead of 50,000 was an amazing miracle? And what if every single one of them was doing their very best to give us all an amazing gift— an amazing wake-up call—in the process?

Yes, I know that many surviving family members, having experienced pain at losing their loved ones might initially scoff at this concept, and I totally understand that and them. What I am trying to do is present a different explanation that might give all of us—even the family members left behind—a greater level of peace and awareness.

Let me try to explain a bit more.

What would it take for you to realize that there are choices that you make as a being that go far beyond your cognitive understanding? If every choice that you are making didn't have to have cognitive understanding or cognitive awareness, would you have more choice available? And, would you recognize that you were choosing even when you were not cognitive about it?

What if there was something that the people in the buildings and the planes knew that goes far beyond this reality? What if they truly are infinite beings, which means their awareness goes far beyond just this reality and its limited awareness and limited choices? What if, on some level, they knew they could make a contribution to CHANGING THE WORLD? What if the way they chose to do it was allowing their bodies to die that day so they could wake other people (us) up?

The world changed that day. You can argue that it has changed for the worse. That could be true. Or, is it possible that the world would have been much worse if 9/11 had never occurred? What if it was a wake-up call, forcing people into the awareness that change is necessary? What if it was part of the demand for more consciousness? And what if every single person that chose to allow their body to die that day contributed to that awareness FOR THE WORLD.

My question is, does it make you feel lighter?

I know of people whose alarm didn't go off that morning. Or they got in a taxi and got stuck in rush-hour traffic. Or their kid was sick. Or they just got a clear message that they needed to turn around and not go to those buildings that day ... Literally, what if this is what the people created who were choosing something other than to die that day? What if those people knew that the greatest gift they could be was to stick around? What if there's something much larger going on than we have been willing to consider? Once again, what's true for you makes you feel lighter. What makes YOU feel lighter?

One interesting thing that occurred directly after 9/11 is that New Yorkers invited total strangers into their homes, caring for them, rather than fearing for their lives or possessions. That had not been the case in New York city since the 60s. The city banded together in a show of caring and solidarity that was unlike anything the city had EVER experienced. Would you consider that a gift?

One other interesting thing that I have noticed: when asking many people when they started on their journey of exploring possibilities beyond this reality, many of them tell me that they started exploring in 2001 or 2002 or 2003, the very years after 9/11. Coincidence? Maybe. And maybe the people who were brave enough to change that day really had the effect they were looking to have.

And please understand, I am not talking about a cognitive choice!

"If I hide maybe I won't die."

There seems to be two common ways where people decide on something that sets their body on the path toward death. One is where you decide when you are young that you won't live past a certain age. It's just a decision. Then you get past that age and your life stops because you thought you were going to be dead, so you projected enough life to that point. And then you prepare to die. Weird, eh?

Do YOU have a drop-dead date?

I'd like to tell you about someone we'll call Cynthia. She was 54 years old when I met her—and absolutely nothing in her life worked. I asked her a lot of questions and finally we found the limitation that literally was killing her. And I have to tell you, this was a surprise to me.

When Cynthia was around three years old, she had decided that she wasn't going to live past 51. And everything in her life slipped out of her hands when she turned 51. She stopped making money, she stopped having friendships—everything just stopped.

Fifty-One was her expiration date.

Do you have an expiration date when your body is supposed to kick off? At what age? Do you see the insanity in that point of view? For example, Cynthia made this decision at three years old. What exactly does a three-year-old know about death and aging and when they would like to die? This is another example of a totally non-cognitive choice that was having a huge affect in someone's life.

If you have one of these drop-dead dates, would you please now destroy and uncreate everything you aligned and agreed with and resisted and reacted to that allows it to exist? Right and Wrong, Good and Bad, POD and POC, All Nine, Shorts, Boys and Beyonds.™ *Thank you.*

But Wait, There's More....

The other common way to set your body on a path toward death is if you're in a relationship or some situation that you want to get out of, and so you go, "Oh, I'm dead," or "I just want to die."

And you make the decision to die so that you can get out of it. You set your body on the death course, and it becomes really tough for you to have a life and for you to have any form of abundance. It is weird, I know. Really weird.

Let me give you an example. Gary was working with a woman in her 70s who had been diagnosed with breast cancer. He asked her, "What are you dying to get out of?"

She answered, "My relationship."

Gary asked her, "Have you considered getting a divorce?"

She replied, "Oh no. I could never do that to my children!"

He asked, "How old is your youngest child?"

She said, "54."

No matter how hard Gary tried, she was totally unwilling to change her point of view. He gave her money back and told her he couldn't help her. She died of breast cancer.

Most people think—If I hide maybe I won't die.

No, actually if you choose to live, then you won't die! I know, like many other things we've already covered, it's weird.

First, you have to undo the decision to die, IF YOU ARE WILLING TO. (That, by the way, is exactly what the clearing statement is for—undoing the yuck that you've had no way to undo until now.) Second, you have to actually make the choice to truly live. (A lot of people have trouble getting past disease processes, poverty and depression because they haven't yet chosen TO LIVE.)

And look, if any of this is light to you, is it time to choose differently now?

To choose living?

For those of you that know this applies and would like to change it—would you be willing to? Right now?

Will you now destroy and uncreate every time you decided to die, and that you wanted to die to get out of something? And everything that doesn't allow that, let that go now, please? And will you now make the choice and the demand to live? No matter what that looks like and no matter what it takes?

And everything that doesn't allow that, let's destroy and uncreate that now, please? Right and Wrong, Good and Bad, POD and POC, All Nine, Shorts, Boys and Beyonds.™ *Thank you.*

Thank you. From me, and your body.

(By the way, just check in with your body right now. Any lighter?)

Let me tell you a story with a happier ending: There was a woman I worked with, let's call her Chandra, who had uterine fibroids, diagnosed by a medical doctor with ultrasound results to prove it. When I asked her, "What's the value in holding on to this?" she realized that it was the only way she knew of healing the people around her. Her body was literally trying to heal others by taking on their pain and disease. (Which is far more common than most people would ever realize.)

With a little questioning, and using the clearing statement to undo where she felt she couldn't do it any other way, and a little ESB work, she was fibroid free. She went back to the ultrasound lab because she was scheduled for surgery to remove the fibroids and wanted to see if there was a change from our session. The ultrasound technician stared in disbelief as he ran the ultrasound wand over her abdomen while looking at the films from the previous scan. He finally pronounced that the first ultrasound must have been wrong because he detected no fibroids. Hehe. :) Happy Chandra!

Somewhere, somehow, in our session, Chandra got what she needed to choose something different. Please know, it's always the person's choice— not mine.

———— SMALL NOTE TO READER ————

You may be wondering how I got to the point where I could trust my awareness about these things that I have shared with you (for example, that Cynthia indeed made the decision to die at 3, or that Chandra was on the right track to changing the fibroids situation). With this, as with everything else, I used the tool I have already shared with you: rocket science.

Oops! Sorry, I forgot, wrong tool. It's much easier than rocket science.

I started with the awareness that something true always makes us feel lighter. And then I just let my mind go and followed whatever came up. And when it created more lightness, I would keep going down that path. When it got heavier, I knew that was not the direction to go in, so I changed directions with my questioning.

And how do I know what I did actually worked and that I wasn't making that up in my head?

BECAUSE CYNTHIA'S LIFE AND CHANDRA'S BODY GOT A LOT BETTER. Cynthia has been creating more and more and more ever since. And her new husband is pretty happy about it too. Chandra's body has been a continual source of amazement and greater joy for her ever since. So please know, the way I know that what I am looking at with someone is actually working is that THE SITUATION ACTUALLY CHANGES.

Though I speak about a lot of weird, different subjects from a very weird, different place, I'm actually very, very pragmatic. If some tool I'm using doesn't work to change something, then I will look for, and often find, a different tool, a different perspective, a different way of looking at things that allows the situation to change. That's how Access has been created over the last 25 years, by working with real people to change real things, whether that thing was changeable yesterday or not—and whether this reality says it's changeable or not.

Remember in the introduction when I brought up the idea of heading in the direction of being able to move our bodies from here to Fiji instantaneously? That's because I've seen person after person after person after person that didn't know a particular change was possible. And through questioning, being open without conclusion, using the clearing statement to undo the points of view keeping limitation in place, they changed the very thing they didn't think was possible to change.

So, my question is, "What else is changeable? What else is possible? What else do we have the capacity to change that we didn't know we had the capacity to change?" And ... "What would it take for all of us to have the tools to change EVERYTHING we'd like to change?" That's what I'm heading for. Wanna play? Change directly ahead....

✑ ✑ ✑

If Death Is Just a Choice, Maybe So Is LIVING....

Let me tell you about a choice I made once ... I was riding in Costa Rica a couple of years back. I was on my beautiful half Costarricense, half Quarter Horse (who's like a rocket on four hooves). He's the fastest horse that I have ever ridden, and I've ridden some pretty fast horses.

So, here we are on this ride, and there is a person that was a beginner that decided he was going in the advanced group. So here he is, directly in front of me. We are going up a six-foot embankment that is pure mud, and the horses have to climb up this embankment to get out of the river.

The newbie-turned-advanced rider manages to get up the embankment, and as soon as he gets to the top, he stops—right in front of me. My horse is in mid-climb at this point, I cannot go any further. And so he now starts to fall over backwards on top of me down a six-foot embankment of mud into three feet of water in large rocks.

And there I was—presented with a choice—a choice between continuing to live—or dying. I knew then that the choice between living and dying was like the snap of a finger. It is so easy to let it all go. I had never experienced that before. When I planned to die just prior to finding Access, I was going to kill myself in six months if my life did not change. Well, here was the chance. I saw it and I knew, "Wow. It's that easy. Oh ... If I chose to, I could just fall backwards now and end it all. ... "

So my choice was: "Yes? No? Yes? No."

"NO!"

I thought, "No, that's not happening right now."

So my horse turned sideways.

Now we are sideways and I think, "Ok, that's better. He's not going to fall over backwards on top of me." Only now, he is coming down sideways on top of me. Just before I went totally under water, and just before he landed on me, my back was on the rocks, and I've got my feet up. Like I'm going to do a leg press of a thousand-pound horse? He starts falling over on top of me and again I'm saying, "No." Literally, my body goes (whoosh) and the horse goes (whoosh). It doesn't actually fall in any way that makes sense.

I get up out of the water that I've been submerged in and he's standing there. He struggles and he gets up, and I think, "Ok. I changed something." The people behind me said, "That was really bizarre, you fell but your body was over here, then he fell but he didn't fall here, he fell and went over there, then did this flip thing. ... "

One woman who observed the whole incident while riding behind me said that at one point when I was submerged, my horse, as he was getting up, stepped so close to my head that it looked like he was going to step on it. In her words, his first step in righting himself placed his hoof within "an inch of your head."

My reply to her was: "I'll take it! An inch is all I needed! How does it get any better than that?"

That inch was the difference between life and death. It was just an inch, and it was plenty. I realized then that those are the moments of choice. It is that quick. Only I did not think, "Now, I will flip my body and I will flip my horse."

I just went, "This is going to change. I am not dying today."

That was it. I am still getting awarenesses from that event. Because of it, I had to look and realize, "Ok, I did have the choice to go. I chose not to." And—"If I chose to stick around, I better make something out of my life. If I can change this, what else is possible?" It placed a demand in my world that I create something greater than I had until that point, because if I was not going to create something greater, why stay alive?

Please know, regardless of what space you are stepping into being aware of right now, just by reading this book—that space is a possibility that will continue to grow.

You will give yourself the chance. You will give yourself the possibility.

It does not mean you almost have to die.

It could mean you wake up, thinking, "You know what? Smallness is not enough anymore. Thank you very much world. Bring on something greater!" It does not have to be a big significance. This event happened, piecing it together later, I realized all that happened. None of it was cognitive, other than I realized, "Wow! I made the choice to live."

A New Paradigm for Choice

Truly, it's all choice.

For example, in looking at, "I'm angry because my husband left me" you're assuming that your husband left you, you're assuming it's a bad thing, and you're assuming that you now have a problem based on it. Right?

And in essence, putting yourself in the role of victim.

WARNING: This next section may not be easy for you to believe.

You may find you want to throw the book away.

(Again?)

Please know I would find this very hard to believe too if I hadn't lived it just as I have described it here. It may challenge every paradigm you've ever had and every concept of what you have considered true in the past. I'm not asking you to believe me.

I'm asking you to open up your world to a different possibility, one which may give you more freedom to know what you know, regardless of whether it goes against everything your past and those around you have told you is real, necessary or true. And in so doing, hopefully you will find more of what is true for you.

And if any of what you read here makes you feel lighter, you may find it "frees" you, in some way you can't explain and don't "understand." If so, my willingness to expose this part of my life to you has been worthwhile.

Here goes:

When I was a kid, I experienced many forms of abuse—sexual abuse, physical abuse, emotional abuse and fearing for my life. An older relative molested me, and I was also molested by an older boy. I also experienced being beaten with belts—my little naked boy body was beaten with belts by a circle of women who hated men, standing over me doing that. There were other forms of abuse I experienced in childhood that I won't go into here, but I think you get the idea.

In some of the metaphysical work I did about six years prior to coming into contact with Access Consciousness, I had the awareness that I had been abused ... I went, "Oh my God! That explains it."

That explained every limitation for me. That explained why I wasn't willing to feel good about myself, why I wasn't able to make lots of money, why I felt like crap, why I didn't like myself very much. It explained everything to me. I went, "Wow, now I see why I am a victim. Ok, good." Exactly. Where could I go from there?

I was functioning from conclusion rather than question.

So after about a year and a half in Access, Gary Douglas (the founder of Access) and I started looking at this area of abuse that I had undergone. I started telling him what I perceived had occurred, but I felt like there was a lot of it that I had blocked off.

Initially, we looked at it from the point of view that everybody else on this planet has, which is the psychological point of view, which is, "That's a badness. That's a wrongness. And I'm a victim." And believe me, I understand that point of view. The biggest difficulty with that point of view is that it too is a conclusion rather than a question. You shut off any other possibility that could exist. You shut the other doors of possibility and limit yourself to only being aware of what you've already concluded.

We were looking from the point of view of wrongness, and trying to clear it. Not much was happening except that Gary and I were getting more awareness of the things that had occurred for me, because I would get a little glimpse, and share it.

I say again, because we had decided it was wrong that I had experienced what I had, we couldn't see anything other than the wrongness of the situation. Have you ever been in a situation like that in your life—where there seemed to be no lightness? If so, you know what it's like to be in that place.

One night we started processing, and we were actually getting into more of what had occurred. I didn't see it, but Gary got a download of the abuse and the molestation that my body and I had experienced. His point of view was, "That should never happen to a child."

Notice that is an appropriate point of view, but it's not a question. So he went into the wrongness of what had been done to me. In that very point of view, he saw me as a victim, and he made me a victim, because he aligned and agreed with the point of view that I was a victim in that situation. That locked my body and me up.

Please know I am not blaming him. I am telling you this so you can see what we do to stick ourselves (and others) with a point of view of wrongness or being a victim. And, you'll soon see what we did to change it.

I felt like I was covered in concrete that had just solidified. I could hardly move. My bowels stopped. I didn't even know what happened. I thought, "This abuse is really kicking in."

No.

What had really happened was that Gary took a point of view that it was a wrongness, and that stuck me with it. He didn't function as the question at that point, though he almost always does. Because he concluded this was something that was so horrendous that should never happen, he couldn't see anything that didn't match that conclusion. It's like looking at 9/11 as only a wrongness. If you do, you can't ever see that there may be some different possibility lurking there, waiting to make your reality easier, greater, with more possibilities.

I got stuck with the idea that I had undergone something that was so horrendous it should never happen, and I was the victim of it, and it was more powerful than me.

If I was the victim of it, which makes all that energy greater than me, it meant I couldn't be greater than even that energy of abuse. That's really a tough place to function, because if you can't get greater than the energy of abuse, you don't have much possibility in your life. And I didn't. Literally it felt like my life stopped.

Please get this: your point of view creates your reality.

Even if somebody else puts a point of view on you and you buy it, it determines your reality. I wasn't cognitively aware of it. The thing is, most of what occurs for us is non-cognitive. What happened was that Gary had the point of view that this shouldn't happen to a child and that I was a victim. And I already had the point of view that I was a victim, because that's the point of view people have about abuse here –that you're a victim. My point of view of being a victim combined with his point of view that I was a victim to that circumstance stuck my life.

So here I was, in the most solid concrete of my life, and neither Gary nor I knew where to go, nor what to do about it.

We didn't know what had happened to stick me. We just knew we got somewhere, and something happened. When we get somewhere and we don't know what's going on, we start asking questions.

Quite frankly, I started getting really, really angry. And much of it I was directing at Gary, my best friend. It wasn't my best choice, and I'm not proud of it—but with his utter kindness with me, no matter how angry I got, and with his amazing level of allowance for me (and everyone) no matter what—we got through it. Since then, I realized that when I'm getting angry at the people I care about, I'm stuck in some old pattern that goes beyond my cognitive thinking, or there's actually a level of ability to change something I am stepping into that I've never experienced before.

So Gary was asking me questions, and asking me questions—but they were still all from the point of view that everybody has here, that it was a wrongness, and that I was a victim. We kept going, "What's wrong?" Or, in an effort to look at something different that might "unstick" me, we would shift to, "What else could be wrong that we haven't looked at yet?"

Notice the point of view we were functioning from: something is wrong. With that point of view, could we ever see anything else than some form of wrongness? No. And every time you ask, "What's wrong?" you look for what's wrong. In fact that's all you can see. The question we weren't asking about this was, "What might be right about this that we are not getting?"

What we did know was that if you keep going to work on something and it doesn't clear or doesn't change, you're not looking at the right thing. Get this, if things don't get lighter, there's some other way of looking at things. What's true always makes you feel lighter. When you get to that thing that is true, it will create lightness in even the heaviest situation. As long as things are still heavy, there's a lie in there somewhere. So Gary asked the question of himself, "What is the lie here?"

Further, he used the clearing statement. Every time he would ask, "What's the lie here?" he would then ask to destroy and uncreate everything that allowed the lies to stay in place and everything that didn't allow him to perceive what was actually true and what would create freedom for me. And then he would say, "Right and Wrong, Good and Bad, POD and POC, All Nine, Shorts, Boys and Beyonds.™"

(Talk about a really, really good friend!)

After doing this for several days, he asked me a question that changed my whole life. He said, "I know it's going to sound strange, but did you have anything to do with creating this?"

I took a deep breath. It was the first thing that had lightened my universe in eight weeks. Quite frankly, I was astonished. I didn't think I was ever going to get through the concrete wall around me. And there it was: a ray of lightness!

Remember that something that's true always makes you feel lighter? I said, "Oh my God. I had something to do with creating it." ONLY because it brought so much lightness to my world after so much heaviness had been there. And quite frankly, I have to tell you, I would probably not have believed that I had ANYTHING to do with creating those situations that occurred in my childhood if I had not experienced the weeks of heaviness followed by instantaneous lightness when Gary asked me that question. And I completely understand if this conversation is bringing up things for you or "pushing your buttons." I can only imagine how it would be for me if I were reading about it right now rather than having experienced it, just as I am writing it.

Please, just read on....

I had no idea what it was that I had to do with creating the situation, but just that awareness that I had something to do with creating it allowed me to start, even in the slightest way, to come out of being a victim.

I had had this point of view in my universe that the abuse that occurred was a wrongness, and that I was a walking wrongness for allowing it. I knew it. Everybody knows that, don't they? Guess what? That's one of the ways in which this reality, and its limited point of view about abuse, limits us. What if that's not the only possible option to consider?

We have this collective unconscious point of view that abuse is something that is only done TO SOMEONE, and you are a terrible victim, and these wonderful things that perpetrate total impotence on anybody who has ever experienced any of it.

What if that's not the only perspective we can take? What if taking only that point of view is not a kindness to the beautiful being that experiences abuse? What if the people who experience abuse are some of the bravest beings on the planet? What if they have courage beyond anyone's ability to express in words?

When Gary said, "Did you have anything to do with creating it?" my universe went boom! It was like fireworks -s-p-a-c-e- for the first time in eight weeks. I could feel the concrete block lifting....

The he asked me another question, "Did you do this on purpose?"

All the rest of the concrete blocks blew off—BOOM!—and I started laughing and crying at the same time. That made no sense to me. It was so not cognitive that it could be the case, I couldn't figure out how or why or any of that, and I didn't really care. It created so much space that instantaneously, I knew it had to be true. Then he asked, "Why? For what reason did you do this?"

I looked. My eyes crossed, because having to look at that from such a different point of view was such a change for me. He asked, "Did you do it to create change?"

Big YES!

Okay. Gary kept going. "So did you do it to create change for your family, other kids, the man who molested you, all of the above or something else?"

Wow! All of the above.

Suddenly I was able to look at everything that had occurred and have total clarity about it, as though I was watching the situation unfold. What I saw was bizarre and astonishing and totally the opposite of what it appeared to be!

In the case of the older relative, I made it so the family knew about it. I could see that if I didn't do that with him, more likely than not, he would have ended up becoming someone who was sexually inappropriate and doing really unkind and nasty things to other kids, and maybe even go to prison for it. I had changed the course of his life. But perhaps even more importantly, I had changed the course of many childrens' lives in the future.

Now I have had years of looking at things from a different place (which is strange to most people, maybe even you). And still, when this first came up, it blew me away to be able to recognize that at six years old, I was able to make that choice, because of the caring I had for this relative of mine and for the people he would affect.

Caring? That was so far beyond anything I could conceive of as caring at the time. Yet it made me feel light once again, and made everything easier. That is the only litmus test for something you don't understand or have experienced before: does it make you feel lighter? If so, it's true for you, even if you don't understand why.

You see, that's what becoming aware of what's true does for you. Buying a lie always makes you feel heavier and you bury yourself even more, which is where I was just prior to Gary asking me the questions that led to these amazing awarenesses. I looked from this new space back at the child I was, recognizing that caring and the awareness that was there at six years old. I actually knew I had to do this, because if I didn't this guy would end up hurting other kids—and himself.

It was very interesting, to say the least, having this experience. I was able to look at everything and have total clarity about it as though I was watching the situation unfold. And I knew that I could perceive the future—even at six years old. That realization that I perceived the future AND CHOSE TO CHANGE IT was as jarring as any I have ever had.

Furthermore, when I checked in with my body ... it was actually okay. My amazing, beautiful body was not broken and hurt. It knew how to heal. It had walked with me and had my back. We had more than survived. We had changed something. And we had found our way to the tools that would allow us to thrive. That day expanded into an appreciation of my body that was greater than anything I thought possible up until that point.

I'm sorry—tell me how I'm a pathetic victim again, please?

One of the most important things here is to realize that no matter what you have experienced, you too, will find your way to the tools that will allow you to thrive, whatever they may be for you. They are available. JUST DON'T STOP. YOU CAN DO THIS.

The realizations I shared above changed my life. Everything changed that day—everything. It was then I came out of buying what this reality tells us is true as though it is. It was then that I came out of the reverence for this reality, and everything that it says, and everything that it is. From my point of view, that's really all that matters.

It's not about fighting this reality.

It's like when you're in a relationship somebody has been lying to you the whole time and you get to the point where you have had enough, and you say—"Do whatever you need to. It's totally fine, but I'm done with you lying to me. I'm done. Our relationship as it was is now over. I don't know what the future will bring, but our relationship is now over."

My relationship with this reality became over that day. It's been an amazing journey of—"What else is possible? What else is possible? What else is possible?"

When I asked that question in the past, it was always somehow couched in the terms of, "What else is possible IN THIS REALITY?" That day, with the awarenesses I had, it changed.

From then on, asking, "What else is possible?" included choices that were not ever possible before that.

This is very important. Please, I am absolutely not saying that abuse is a rightness. My personal point of view is that there is no reason to ever abuse anyone or anything. It goes against our very nature as beings. It is one of the insanities on this planet that I would love to have cease to exist.

Not only that, I am doing everything I can to give everyone the tools to change this. It is something I would stop in almost any way I could if someone I knew were experiencing it.

Please also realize, if it has occurred for you or someone you love, seeing them as a victim could be the most unkind thing you could do to them. Seeing them as a powerful, potent being who MAY have chosen it to change someone's life may unlock them from the stigma of victim under which they have been living.

Abuse occurs. What we choose to do about it will determine the course of someone's life in their future. And, what if part of our purpose here is to create a world where abuse cannot exist. What if that's part of why we're here. If we're going to create that as a reality, we truly need to function from a DIFFERENT point of view than what we have decided is real in the past.

What we have decided is real in the past has given us the world we currently have. We need something DIFFERENT to create a DIFFERENT WORLD.

If you or someone you know has experienced abuse, I am not saying you're at fault for it occurring. At all. If you have been abused, YOU ARE NEVER AT FAULT.

The act of abuse is always inappropriate. You are not wrong because you experienced it. You are not bad because you experienced it. You don't have to be a victim any longer because you experienced it. You have courage beyond your wildest imaginings. The fact that you could experience abuse and still function and create a life is a testament of your courage, and ability and your capacity. You are far greater than you know—far, far greater.

Everything that doesn't allow you to now know that you are greater than even the abuse you have experienced, in whatever form that has taken, will you now please destroy and uncreate it? Right and Wrong, Good and Bad, POD and POC, All Nine, Shorts, Boys and Beyonds.™ Thank you.

Please try on these perspectives to see if they make you feel lighter. Please don't buy whatever you think is my point of view. I don't have a point of view, other than I would like to see you be as free, happy and easily amazing as you truly be. And remember, what's true always makes you feel lighter. A lie always makes you feel heavier.

You could start with these really simple questions if you or someone you know has experienced abuse:

1. What lies am I buying about this that are sticking me?

2. What do I know about what occurred that I have been pretending not to know or denying that I know?

3. What other ways can I look at this situation to create freedom for me (or the person that has been abused)?

4. Is there any way in which I have protected someone or changed someone's life by allowing this to occur?

5. What courage, potency and capacity do I have that allowed me to survive this abuse that I haven't been acknowledging, that if I would acknowledge it would set me free?

Almost no one else I know of on the planet is willing to look from this different place of possibility regarding abuse. Because of the unique circumstances of my life, I have been fortunate to discover and help bring to light this totally different perspective. It has literally given me— and hundreds, if not thousands of others—freedom where nothing else (psychology, metaphysics, various other techniques too numerous to mention, including religion) had.

That is the reason I have been willing to expose this area of my life to you—so that you and the people you love know there is a different possibility. Whether you choose to look from this place is, as always, your choice. Please, as always, choose that which makes you feel lighter.

Again, please know, I am not saying that same scenario is true for everybody that experienced abuse. What I am saying is that looking from a different perspective can often create a different possibility than anyone ever imagined.

What might be uncovered in your life if you didn't look for the wrongness of the events of your past but instead asked, "What's right about me that I am not getting?" and "What do I know that I'm pretending not to know?" and "What different perspective can I look from that will create space, ease, and freedom around the situation?" That's what I have learned to do, and it works wonders to open up different possibilities that I never considered could exist.

See, all of this is about making your life and this world a BETTER place to live. It's not just to buy a fixed point of view and stick with it. It's about creating a different reality, not continuing to create the same limited reality THAT DOESN'T WORK!

It's time for change. It's time for difference.
It's time for you to be free.
It's time for us all to be free.

What if you are far more potent and amazing than you have ever given yourself credit for? What might change in your life if you acknowledged that?

What if you no longer had to fear death?

Do YOU really die? Or is it just your body that dies?

Think about it for a moment.

Are you an infinite being?
Or are you just a body?

Or are you an infinite being who created (along with Universal Intelligence, God, Consciousness, or whatever you want to call it) your sweet body?

And if that is the case, is it possible YOU don't die?
Is it possible only your body does, in prelude to changing form?
Is it possible you have other choices after your body dies? Other glorious possibilities?

Would that put you more at ease about this thing called dying?
What if that, too, were something totally different than you thought it was?
Surely, you've heard this idea before....

Even if your background is that of religion, where you believe in a supreme being ... and a Heaven and a Hell.

If you're going to Heaven (hopefully), is the thing that enters Heaven your body ... or you the being? I would venture to say you, the being, since by all accounts, your body is hanging out here after you're gone.

Let me give you an example: There was a preacher's wife who came to a class my friend and founder of Access, Gary Douglas, was offering. Referring to a child she knew that had recently passed at three days old, she said to Gary, "You know, I didn't believe in all this past life stuff, but I guess you're correct. We must live on after we die. God wouldn't create a soul to last only three days. I wonder what's next for me?"

And, dear reader, if you don't have to fear dying anymore, because you, the being, don't die, I wonder … what could be next for you?

Here and now, in this body, on Earth: what is next for you?

Fear Is Always a Lie

Please know that fear, for an infinite being, is always a lie. It's always a lie.

Always a lie.

One more time—fear is always a lie.

Fear is either somebody else's point of view or it's an implanted point of view designed to not get you to look at what you'd really like to look at that can change your reality. It's designed to keep you from looking at what's underneath what you're calling the fear, which is where you, the being, actually are.

Fear can also be excitement that you've misidentified and misapplied. Most of us have actually done this. Fear and excitement are physiologically very similar. And most people have misidentified that wonderful energy of excitement (when our heart speeds up, our breathing increases, and we somehow become more acutely aware) as fear.

Let me give you an example: When Gary was a little kid of about six years old, he was going to go on the Ferris wheel with his mom for the first time. He was SO EXCITED that he was jumping up and down while holding her hand. She looked down and said, "Now don't be afraid, dear."

From that point forward, whenever he had that excited feeling, he assumed what he was having was fear—until he found this information. Now, he asks, "Is this fear or excitement?" Hint: It hasn't ever been fear since he started asking this question 23 years ago.

How much of what you've been calling fear is actually excitement you've misidentified and misapplied? Everything that is will you destroy and uncreate it please? Right and Wrong, Good and Bad, POD and POC, All Nine, Shorts, Boys, and Beyonds.™

Would you like me to prove to you that you don't truly have fear?
OK, what happens to you in an emergency situation? Do you fall apart?

No, you get calm, cool and collected, and you handle the situation, right?
Good, then you don't truly have fear. Now you may fall apart afterwards to
prove that you were indeed fearful like everybody else says you're supposed
to be. If you believe you have fear, run these processes over and over and it
will (if you're willing) change.

*What's the value of functioning from the lie that you have fear instead of choice? Everything
that is, would you uncreate and destroy all of that please? Right and Wrong, Good and
Bad, POD and POC, All Nine, Shorts, Boys and Beyonds.*™

*What's the value of functioning from the lie that you are afraid to choose? Everything that
is, would you uncreate and destroy all of that please? Right and Wrong, Good and Bad,
POD and POC, All Nine, Shorts, Boys and Beyonds.*™

*What's the value of always having fear rather than the total excitement of choice and
choosing? Everything that is, would you uncreate and destroy all of that please? Right
and Wrong, Good and Bad, POD and POC, All Nine, Shorts, Boys and Beyonds.*™

When you go into fear you take yourself right out of choice. Have you ever
noticed that? That's its job. To get you to stop choosing to move forward.

Are you going to let the little, limiting lie called fear win? When you come
up against fear, are you willing to make a different choice? ANY different
choice?

Here's a three-step process for eliminating fear from your life, but you have
to use it when the fear comes up instead of letting the lie that you have fear
paralyze you.

1. Ask, "Who does this belong to?" If it gets lighter, it's not yours. Return
    to sender.

2. Ask, "Is this fear or excitement?" If it's excitement, then celebrate!

3. POD and POC all of the distractor implants creating the "fear."

If you do these three things every time fear comes up, you will eventually be free of it.

Fear is one of the excuses, one of the reasons and justifications that no one can argue with. Because everybody else also considers it real, you can say, "I didn't do this because I was afraid" and everybody immediately says, "Oh I know what you're talking about." They use it as the validation that fear is real in their own worlds too.

What if you were willing to be something that's completely different? When I do classes I talk to people about the things I've gotten into that weren't smart and weren't bright. I tell them about the places where I had something that was like fear and somehow found a way to change it. I want them to know, "Yes, I've gone through this too, and I totally get you. And, there's a different possibility available."

Let me ask you a question:

Are you willing to be that different possibility?

Let me ask you another question:

Do you know that you are a different possibility already? Have you been trying to pretend that you're not? Everything you've been doing to try to pretend you are not the different possibility that can exist beyond fear, will you destroy and uncreate it please? Right and Wrong, Good and Bad, POD and POC, All Nine, Shorts, Boys and Beyonds.™ *Thank you.*

JUST AN IPOV … *Meet Forrest Gump*

Would you like a life of total ease? If there were one big key to getting you there, faster, more completely, and with more ease than any other, this would be it. Let me introduce you to your new best friend, the famous Russian: JUSTAN IPOV.

This simply means that you allow every point of view, whether yours or someone else's, to be <u>JUST AN</u> <u>I</u>nteresting <u>P</u>oint <u>O</u>f <u>V</u>iew (JUSTAN I.P.O.V.).

This is also known as being in ALLOWANCE. It sounds pretty simple, right?

Please know this: **your point of view creates your reality. Reality does not create your point of view.** So, if you have no judgment in your point of view, you will have no limitation in how your reality can show up, because judgment is the great limiter. For every judgment we have, nothing that does not match that judgment can show up in our world.

Have you ever noticed that even when the exact same situation happens to people, different people have different points of view about it? Some have judgments about the situation, which always feel heavy. Some people are in allowance, which always has a lightness to it. It's just their choice.

JUSTAN IPOV is a way of choosing to change your point of view—from one of judgment (and limitation) to one of allowance (and possibilities).

My friend, Gary, saw a television news program after Hurricane Andrew hit Florida. On that program there was a man in his underwear, whose house had literally been blown away in the hurricane. He said to the news reporter, *"I moved here to retire, bought this house with my retirement money and had everything*

I owned in it. Now, it's all gone. All I have is this slab of concrete [meaning the concrete foundation]. *But, I'm still alive, and I managed to salvage a pair of underwear, so I'm doing pretty good."*

In other words, this man was functioning from it being an interesting point of view that his house had blown away. He was in total allowance.

On that same program, there were numerous people who saw themselves as totally devastated, even though they had much more left in terms of wordly possessions than this man had. What's the difference? Their point of view. The people who saw themselves as devastated were NOT functioning from interesting point of view. They were not functioning from allowance. They were in judgment, and their reality reflected that. They were VERY UPSET.

Who do you suppose had an easier time moving on and creating a new life after Hurricane Andrew, the man in allowance or the people in huge amounts of judgment? Most likely the man in allowance.

What's the difference? It's their choice of point of view. If a hurricane blew your house away, what point of view would you rather choose? Which would work better FOR YOU? Gratitude that you survived, or anger and hatred that your house didn't?

If you feel like you're not one of those people that would be able to be grateful to be alive if a hurricane took your house away, that's OK. That's not the point. The point is that there is a way to get there if you want it. That's what all the tools in this book are about.

Think of Forrest Gump. For him, magic just kept happening because he was in total allowance of everything. His life was magic because he didn't limit the possibilities of what could show up for him by judging anything. You could say he wasn't smart enough to judge. Maybe he was smart enough NOT to.

This is why I say, *"Your point of view creates your reality. Reality does not create your point of view."* If you chose to function from no judgment, your life could show up more like Forrest Gump's. Does that sound like more fun?

As an example, here are a few different points of view and the reality that gets created from them. I'm sure you could add many more of your own:

Point of view: I'm grateful to be alive.

Reality created: A life worth being grateful for.

Point of view: I'm angry at the world for letting a hurricane blow my house away.

Reality created: Many, many reasons to have increasing amounts of anger at the world, at God, at the Earth and everyone on it. Since you are included in the world, you don't get spared the anger either. Many people with these points of view experience things like the insurance company not paying for a very long time, or they unexpectedly find out that their policy was not in effect during the hurricane—all more reasons and justifications to get even angrier and see themselves as right in the first place for having chosen to get angry. It becomes a vicious cycle.

Point of view: I have to work hard for money.

Reality created: Money never comes easy, and it always seems to be a struggle to just get by. (If you could change that point of view, money could show up a lot easier.)

Please know this:

1. The point of view you take is always your choice.

2. Changing it to something different because it works better for you is also your choice.

3. You don't ever have to be stuck with the point of view you currently have—about anything.

4. The tools in this book, including JUSTAN IPOV, allow you to change your points of view easily and painlessly. And when these points of view change, the space of a new possibility becomes available to you.

In other words, one person can experience a hurricane blowing away their house and be grateful to be alive, and another person can be furious with the world for allowing it to happen. Magic happens when you are able to change your point of view from the limited, judgmental point of view to a more expansive point of view—for you.

When you change your points of view, your reality will change as well.

Then, watch out world! You may go around destroying limited points of view around you—just because you can. And as you do, you'll inspire others to know it's possible. And as you do, the world we live in will change.

The easiest way to change any situation is to change your point of view surrounding the situation. When you change your point of view, the situation around you literally changes to match your new point of view.

Let's explore a different situation where JUSTAN IPOV saved the day.

I was working with a woman who wanted to get over her feelings of jealousy regarding her mate. She was convinced that her mate wanted to be with someone else. This feeling was consuming her, eating at her almost every moment of the day and night, and she didn't know what to do about it.

Partially because I didn't know where else to start at the time, I asked her to do this exercise—even if she didn't believe it. I asked her to say, "interesting point of view I have this point of view" three times. She did and began to feel lighter. So I had her say it over and over again many more times. At a certain point she started to giggle.

When I asked her what was so funny, she said, *"That I would have a neurotic point of view like this when I love this woman so much! That's not love! And I'm over it! And, if she wants to be with someone else, I now know that I would be just fine. Not that I want that to happen, but if it does, I will be OK. Very interesting."*

What was even more interesting to me is the story the woman related to me a week later in a phone call. She said, *"It was the most amazing thing! My girlfriend came home after I did the 'USTAN IPOV' session with you and was excited to speak with me. She said, 'I have been wanting to tell you this for so long but I never felt I could for some reason: I love you so much and I adore you so much! I am so grateful to be with you! I don't know why I couldn't tell you before, but I'm so glad I can let it be known now. Thank you for being with me. I feel like the luckiest girl in the world!'*

What was the one thing that changed to create that result? The woman's point of view. Because your point of view creates your reality, when she changed her point of view, her reality changed. As she got into allowance of her partner leaving if she needed to, it gave her partner the freedom to CHOOSE to stay and to be grateful for her.

If you'd like total freedom from all limitations, including judgment, viewing everything as an INTERESTING POINT OF VIEW can begin to create that. When everything is just an interesting point of view, you are not seeing anything as good, bad, right or wrong. You are not seeing through the eyes of judgment. You don't have to align and agree (positive polarity) or resist and react (negative polarity) to anything.

It is like being the rock in the stream. You are in allowance. You allow all these points of view to come at you and go around you, whether they are yours or someone else's, without getting swept up in the stream of judgment, rightness or wrongness. You are free. Can you see how that would make your life much easier? As always, it's your choice.

So, if you'd like total freedom, remember your new best friend, JUSTAN IPOV. How do you use him?

You have to first CHOOSE to function from interesting point of view, like Forrest Gump, even if you don't think you know how. Then, for every point of view you have, either positive or negative, you can say to yourself, *"Interesting point of view I have that point of view"* even if you don't believe it. Then wait a moment, see how the point of view changes, and then say again to yourself, *"Interesting point of view I have that point of view."* Then wait just a moment and say to yourself again, *"Interesting point of view I have that point of view."* If you want to make it humorous, as I often do, you could say it in your best Forrest Gump voice … and keep "running and running…."

Now see how the point of view "feels" to you. If it's really light, then you're done. If it's lighter but you still have a point of view, try saying it a few more times, pausing after each time. After just a short time of practicing this, most people find that it's much easier to shift points of view than they ever thought it could be.

Would you be willing to use your new best friend, just for tomorrow to try him out? If so, for every point of view you have, just say: *"That's JUSTAN IPOV"* until you don't have a point of view anymore. You will begin to know how easy it can be to change even your own points of view, which are very seldom "interesting" to you.

If you were to do nothing else other than this exercise for every point of view you have for six months, your ENTIRE LIFE would change. Literally.

But we're not going to stop there. There's a lot more in store.

What Defines You?

Who would you be without your name?

If you had no past, what would be possible?

If nothing of you were defined,
what would there be to judge?
Or limit you?

What if **being you** was not a definition,
but a space and a being and a possibility?

Being
—— Undefined ——

How You Be, My Friend?

Are you a bit **uncomfortable?**

Cool, you're in the 'right' place.

Being un-comfortable is actually an awareness that change is underfoot. It's the way you know that the change and difference that you've been asking for is actually being created.

What if that uncomfortableness was one of the greatest rightnesses? It lets you know you are headed in the direction of the difference you were asking for.

Everything you and anybody else in the world around you has done to make you believe that being uncomfortable is a wrongness and that you are wrong, will you uncreate and destroy that now, please? Right and Wrong, Good and Bad, POD and POC, All Nine, Shorts, Boys and Beyonds.™

In other words, it's when something that is totally different than what was your reality before is coming into existence that you feel that amazing discomfort. Because it doesn't come from the same place, it doesn't have any of the same parameters—you don't recognize it, and you can't define it.

So you assume something must be wrong—**and that's actually the new thing showing up.**

My friends, would you be willing to ask this question every time something is uncomfortable?

"Is this actually the difference that I've been asking for showing up in a totally different way than I thought it was going to?"

Would you be willing to be grateful for that?

Just for the next ten seconds?

10

9

8

7

6

5

4

3

2

1

Now breathe....

— Chapter 10 —
Are You Ready to Be Undefined? (And Magical?)

Let's walk in that forest again—no, let's ride through it! (Why do the same thing twice?)

It is fall now. The air is crisp and chilly, and the last rays of the afternoon sun are searching for a place to sleep. The carpet of leaves is thick and soft, red and orange and yellow.

A warm velvet body is moving with you, under the naked branches of the dark trees. The dance of hooves is running through your body, like the current of living. You are the horse, the horse is you, you are the space the horse be, the space the forest be, and the space you be. You have no name, you have no past, and you have no definitions.

In these ten seconds, you have no idea of who you are, or where you are heading. You don't know what it will look like further down the road.

And you have stopped trying to figure it out.

Perceive the magic of that. Just for a few moments ... Riding free ... This is the space of being undefined. It is infinite possibilities.

It is not often chosen in this reality, and therefore it's one of the most uncomfortable places you can be.

It is the place I invite you to explore.

Come with me; let's play the game of getting lost and found.

Many times I have heard people say: *"I feel great when I am in a class. Everything is light, ease, joy and possibilities. Then I go home, and a couple of weeks down the line, it all contracts. I get squeezed back into that box again."*

And I ask; *"Do you get squeezed? Or do you squeeze yourself back in there? Truth?"* More often than not, they laugh from recognition. Again, it is just a choice. Your choice.

You squeeze yourself back into the box.

Do you recognize this? You have this moment of something completely different ... in nature, in class, in lovemaking, in meditation ... this moment of being total space, being undefined, unlimited, and then ... you seem to lose it.

WHAT HAPPENED?

✏ ✏ ✏

Letting Go of the Safety Net

You have been taught to always have a point of view about you. That is your safety and security net: what to accept, what to reject, whom to judge, how to judge you.

It is all conclusions (and judgments). If you are going to change something in your life, then what is required is that you undo all the conclusions in that area that are defining you.

When you do that, you have no idea what is going on. You have no clue— and it is really disconcerting! How does it get even better than that?

Have you ever been there? At a point where you have no idea who you are? And did you automatically think it's a bad thing? What if being undefined were the greatest possibility there is? When you have no idea who you are, then you have to choose to create you and your reality. You can generate anything from this place, since nothing defines you.

Undefined, you are pure magic, my friend. (It just feels really weird....)

⁓ ⁓ ⁓

Truth? Who Am I?

Sometimes you get to this place of un-definition, and you could literally sit on the couch and watch TV all day long, just because....

What happens is that *motivation* starts to go away, and most of the world uses motivation as the driving force for everything they choose; the motivation of not enough money, the motivation of not feeling good about their bodies or themselves, the motivation of feeling lonely, the motivation of fitting in, of winning, of not losing....

When motivation goes away, a lot of what created pain also goes away. And then you are suddenly asking: *"Well, who am I then? What do I do here? What is going on?"*

This is where we squeeze ourselves back into the box, turn our horse and slowly trot away from the forest of difference and possibilities and back to the stable of the normal, average and real of this reality—back to that stale, old, comfortable place—though our Being would rather run free.

We literally uncreate this new space we are becoming by defining and limiting ourselves again. And we have the most impressive and clever strategies for doing so.

Let's look at some of them:

∽ ∽ ∽

Re-Creating Crap

One of the most common, interesting and completely insane strategies we use is to recreate the traumatic and dramatic place we used to function from.

The crap is familiar; in the crap, we know who we are.
(Clever choice.)
It is like we all have our own repetitive pattern that we use to keep ourselves defined and limited.

Do you know exactly what you personally go back to in order to return to the reference points of the Defined You?

"Wow, does it feel good to hate myself this much. I know this!"

"Wow, does it feel good to lose myself in relationship again. I know this!"

"Wow, does it feel good to be so angry that my girlfriend is flirting with someone else. I know this!"

"Wow, does it feel good to feel like I have no money yet again and that I'm struggling against the world yet again. I know this."

Sometimes you are so brilliant that you go back and recreate exactly what you just got out of, for the very reason that if you can get out of it again, then you really got out of it....

Wow! How does it get even more clever than that?

You recreate it to prove that you can get out of it. Or you make sure that you're worthy of the new space by re-creating the limitation and showing your potency in un-creating it again. When you get yourself out of it the second time, you go back and create it a third time.

So how many times do you have to recreate the crap and definitions before you actually allow yourself to have the freedom that you truly be? One, 5, 10, 50, 100, unlimited?

Are you following me? Would you be willing to let that go now? If so, will you destroy and uncreate all of that please? Right and Wrong, Good and Bad, POD and POC, All Nine, Shorts, Boys and Beyonds.™ Thank you.

⌘ ⌘ ⌘

Relationship, Money or Health?

Are you one of those people, who, when you don't know who you are, create a relationship to find out who you are or are not?

Or maybe for you, it is money problems. You know who you are when you have money problems. You've been there, done that; you are an expert on that particular definition.

Or health problems maybe? Whenever things start going really well, you find some way to create: *"Oh yeah, my body is falling apart again."*

Or are you one of those people that is afraid that you will get bored? *Do you really hate not being amused?* Have you decided boredom would be the worst punishment you could ever suffer?

So rather than having everything show up with total ease all the time, you create the stupidity of not being aware. If you had everything showing up with ease and there were no trauma and drama, how bored would you be, and what would you have to work on?

Your point of view is that if you had the ease, joy and glory of living, you'd be so bored you would want to die. Or, maybe you have bought the lie that if you finally got everything handled, then you would just die, because there would be nothing else to do.

With that point of view, no wonder you would want to turn around and trot back to the stable of average, real and normal.

So are you willing to destroy and uncreate all that please?

Right and Wrong, Good and Bad, POD and POC, All Nine, Shorts, Boys and Beyonds.™ *Thank you.*

And explore what really is possible for you?

❧ ❧ ❧

Defined = Defined Receiving

You are more used to being defined and limited. When you are defined, you know what you have to fight, you know what you are willing to receive and what you are willing to refuse—you know your pattern of wrongness. It is so clever.

Why would you choose to be as explosively brilliant and amazing as you truly are?

Why would you choose to be undefined in any way so that no one and nothing would ever own you again? Why?

I say, *"Why not?"*

Or would you?

Even if you'll be totally alone?

If you choose to be undefined, no one else may have the same points of view as you. They may not even be able to find you, let alone the ballpark where you are playing or the universe in which you are living.

This is another of the big things that is going on for all of us. We are not willing to risk being all alone. In this reality, being alone is a wrongness so ugly we don't even want to look at it.

Instead, when we get to a place where we start to occupy too much space, we try to bring ourselves down to a level that is acceptable to other people. We define and limit ourselves to find commonality with everyone else.

How much of that is what you've been doing to validate other people's realities that you are exactly the person that you have proven to them over and over again that you are, that you never were, but that you decided that you are, that they decided you are, that they decided you must be, that you decided you must be, that you never have been but have been trying to be, and don't want to know any different because that would give you no reference points for being?

It would be really bad if you read that again. (And even worse if you actually understood it.)

Everything that is, will you destroy and uncreate it please? Right and Wrong, Good and Bad, POD and POC, All Nine, Shorts, Boys and Beyonds.™ Thank you.

Now, the funny part is that when you're willing to finally take the plunge and be all alone if that's what it takes to have everything you are, more people will want to be around you. You won't be able to get rid of them. You will be so different that they will be attracted to you like moths to a flame. (Think Oprah.)

✍ ✍ ✍

Don't Go Too Far Right, Oh-Oh—or Too Far Left

In order to make your past right, you believe you have to invalidate this new space you are becoming that is different than the past, this space that is going beyond anything you ever thought you could become.

But to make your past right, and to validate everyone else's reality, you must make yourself smaller.

The only way you can maintain your definition of who you are is if you don't change too much.

Only if you don't go too far left, too far right, or too far forward are you able to maintain your definition of you and that everything is okay, normal, average and real.

If you go too far in all directions and expand too much, which is the worst of all things you could do in this reality, and the greatest of all things you could do for creating your own reality, it gets so uncomfortable that you'll do anything you can to go back to the reference points that you know about who you are.

Rather than saying—*enough!*

OK, I may feel like I am totally alone. OK, maybe nobody will have the same points of view as I have, but I am not rolling over anymore! If you don't like me anymore, that is fine. I will love you, care for you, and do anything to facilitate you. And if you don't like me, that is your problem.

Look, there is a beautiful road down there! I am riding there!

You can come with me, or ride beside me, or behind me ... just don't get in my way.

Notice the difference?

You are present in your life.

Are you willing to make that demand?

If you do ... *Is it lighter?*

Everything that doesn't allow that, will you destroy and uncreate all that please? Right and Wrong, Good and Bad, POD and POC, All Nine, Shorts, Boys and Beyonds.™ Thank you.

⌘ ⌘ ⌘

Following the Road of Lightness

This is really how you know you are getting closer to the things that are true for you—you start to get lighter.

When I say that the truth always makes you feel lighter, and a lie makes you feel heavier, it's not just about what people say or do. It is actually when you start going down the path of what's actually true for you, you get lighter and lighter and lighter and lighter.

However, that pretty much *directly contrasts* with everything that everyone here tells you is supposed to make you happy, everything everyone tells you is the way that life has to be here.

Sometimes it is like standing on the edge of a cliff, choosing whether to jump or not.

This reality is the trap that most of us get stuck in. It's kind of like quicksand. It is OK when you just walk on it, but if you stand in it for any amount of time, before you know it you're buried in it, and you're asking: *How did I get buried?*

But now you have the awareness that there is something else. Something that feels lighter. And when everyone else goes into the heaviness and the drama of it all, you can step away from it.

You can ask:

"Hey, is this actually real? Oh, no? Okay, cool. I can step away."

The key part is this: you can step away from it. You have another choice. Then at some point you'll say:

I'm just not going to choose it.

Who cares whether it's real or not?

It's not real for me.

So Here You Are: Becoming Undefined.

Truth, what would you like to choose now? Is it time to generate your living from this unlimited, undefined space?

Just enjoy it—enjoy how very, very uncomfortable it is.

How very, very undefined—and magical?

And, what if it could be comfortable just as easily as uncomfortable? What if you could let what you think is uncomfortable nurture you and grow you.

Truth, my friend?

What else is possible?
How does it get any better than this?

Would an Infinite Being Choose This?

What if you truly are an infinite being?

What if you are limitless and unstoppable?
What if you don't have to function solely from thoughts,
feelings and emotions?

You have choice.

Yes, my dear, you can choose to squeeze yourself
into the box called this reality.

OR

You can function from question, choice and possibility.

You can choose to be vast as the universe.

And vaster.

This is a question that is always relevant:

Would an infinite being truly choose this?
If not, why would you?

PART 2

... *Changing the World*

Please know, I don't desire you to buy my point of view.
Ever.
I know I sound like I do sometimes....

And truly, I don't.

What I would like is for you to be aware of what your point of view is.
I'd like you to be aware of what is true for you.

Whatever that is.

Beautiful You....

I know Part I of this book may have been ... weird. And possibly wonderful, to some of you.

Before you read Part 2 of this book ... (Or have a meeting ... a date ... or go to work ... Really any time you happen to wake up on a given day....)

... TRY THIS:

Everything I've projected or expected this to be, all the judgments, the projections, expectations, separations and rejections about what this is going to be, let's uncreate and destroy all of that now please? Right and Wrong, Good and Bad, POD and POC, All Nine, Shorts, Boys and Beyonds.™

Thank you. Feel that energy?
Light?

And again....

Please say this out loud....

Everything is the opposite of what it appears to be.
Nothing is the opposite of what it appears to be.

Everything is the opposite of what it appears to be.
Nothing is the opposite of what it appears to be.

Everything is the opposite of what it appears to be.
Nothing is the opposite of what it appears to be.

Everything is the opposite of what it appears to be.
Nothing is the opposite of what it appears to be.

Everything is the opposite of what it appears to be.
Nothing is the opposite of what it appears to be.

— Chapter 11 —
Ready to Get Rid
of the Autopilot?

It may seem like it takes so much energy to be present. Initially it does. That's because it's something you haven't done for a very, very long time.

Have you noticed that you've lived most of your life on autopilot checkout.

Here's how it works: when you arrived here, you didn't understand this reality, so you created a mind to give you all the answers of how you could fit in here and be like everyone else. Your mind is always fighting to defend the rightness of this reality, which totally excludes presence. And being. Totally excluding the difference that your reality is.

Say what? YOUR REALITY IS DIFFERENT! I know, it makes no sense. But doesn't it make you feel at least a little bit lighter? That's the reason you so often feel like you're putting your energy into something that isn't working.

Are you aware that this reality is about homogenization? I'm not talking about warming your milk (which would be pasteurization anyway, but shhh …) I'm talking about making you normal, average, real and the same as everyone else.

That, my friend, means not being present as you. That is the autopilot.

So in the beginning it may seem like it takes a lot of energy to be present. … You are fighting your own awareness because you think you have to do something about everything that you now perceive. Then there's a point—if you're actually willing to be present—that instead of taking energy from you, you actually have a lot more energy—and life—available when you turn the autopilot off.

A lot more!

You need less sleep. You eat less. You simply don't require it. It's actually the case of "everything is the opposite of what it appears to be, and nothing is the opposite of what it appears to be" in motion. Now, try figuring that out with your mind!

So everywhere you've decided that being present would take a lot of energy, will you uncreate and destroy all of that now, please? Right and Wrong, Good and Bad, POD and POC, All Nine, Shorts, Boys and Beyonds.™ Thank you.

✑ ✑ ✑

Being the Intensity of You

When you change, your vibration changes as well. The intensity of living gets greater.

It is new for you. It is the unknown.

In an effort to get away from that intensity, you may start eating too much. Or you will call your mother, or get another relationship, or go and have sex with somebody … Or whatever it is for you that you hide behind—or amuse yourself with—to avoid the intensity you are becoming.

You have to be willing to have the intensity if you are going to have the change for which you are asking.

That intensity may often be very, very uncomfortable. But just because it's uncomfortable doesn't mean it's wrong. In fact, the greater the change you've just chosen, the more uncomfortable it may seem for a while.

I'm not saying that anything you might choose in your life is a bad thing or a wrong thing (including something to diminish the intensity you are becoming). By all means, do it if it works for you. Really.

What I am saying is to please ask yourself:

Am I doing this to lower my vibration and my intensity?
Am I doing this to occupy less space? (Or is it going to generate more space for me?)
Am I doing this to feel more comfortable? Am I doing this to feel like I did before?
Will choosing this lead to less fun or more fun in my life?

All you need to do is ask a question.
All it requires is a question.
All it ever requires is a question.

Then, of course, you may want to receive the awareness you get from asking the question ... and even follow it ... Oh, but that might lead to too much fun—really—and that could be bad.

✥ ✥ ✥

What Are Your Real Priorities?

We all have these priorities in our lives that are how we run our lives—and most of us aren't even aware of what they are.

For example, one of the things I've seen with my friend, Gary, is, for him, life is just ease. No matter what. No matter what's going on, no matter what the situation is, there's always a sense of ease going on for him.

Partially, it's because he has these priorities that are what guide his life. He always knows where to put his energy. He's not spinning his wheels putting his energy in places that have no value and aren't going to do something to increase the quality of his life, his living of it, or his consciousness.

You also have priorities that run your life, my friends. The thing is, you usually have no clue of what they truly are. You may think you do....

And my question is: Do you actually know what's valuable to you? What do you actually, truly prioritize in your life?

Would you be willing to make a list?

Right now?

Please read the question twice!

On what did you spend most of your time, energy, thoughts and emotions for the last 7 days?

1. _____

2. _____

3. _____

4. _____

5. _____

Those five things are your ACTUAL priorities. Not the official ones you thought you had.

Yeah. I know.

Interesting choice, right?

Now, what if you asked yourself:

If I could wave my magic wand and have priorities that would contribute to my life, and give me the life I'd really like to have, which of the above would I keep? Which would I throw away? And then....

What five priorities would contribute to generating, creating and instituting the life and living I would truly like to have?

1. _____

2. _____

3. _____

4. _____

5. _____

Now, please POC and POD everything that doesn't allow that those show up with ease for you.

Making People Happy!

Interestingly enough, we also have hidden priorities ... like maintaining ourselves in this reality, never going beyond our family, never hurting other people's feelings—expansive things like that!

For me, making other people happy was one of my major hidden priorities. I had done it my entire life—I tried and tried and tried to make people happy.

It doesn't work very well by the way, but I tried. And I didn't realize that it was my number one priority—my number one hidden priority—for a very long time. I was just bound and determined to do it at all costs.

I had to create a place in my world where I had, number one, to be aware of everybody else's unhappiness and number two, judge it as a wrongness or not something they would choose, and number three, do everything I could to change it.…

I never asked questions like: "Do they really desire to be happy? Is that what they would choose?"

In my autopilot setting, I was actually solidifying their choice with my judgment, and I was also disempowering them with my superiority. Nice, huh?

Is that truly a kindness to me or them? No. Is it bright? No!

What hidden priorities do you have that, while unacknowledged, maintain and entrain what you cannot change and choose as living in ease, joy and exuberant expression and abundance? Will you uncreate and destroy all of that now please? Right and Wrong, Good and Bad, POD and POC, All Nine, Shorts, Boys and Beyonds.™ Thank you.

Oh … I Know You!

You stepped straight into the wrongness of you, didn't you? You came to the conclusion that you've chosen the WRONG priorities! Even the hidden ones are your fault, aren't they? Darn humanoid!

Let me give you another possibility, my friend.

What if you could be grateful for having chosen every single priority in your life? Any choice you're willing to be grateful for creates ease and the possibility of something different showing up.

I am willing to have an experience of screwing something up and talking about it to let people know that I am not necessarily bright. And I am willing to change it and function differently.

Acting perfect, acting like you don't ever have any problems or issues, and acting like you don't ever have anything come up … Does that make you feel lighter? Or is it just a lot of heavy work?

Isn't that just another autopilot?

What if you didn't have to try to prove you were perfect anymore and acknowledge that you already are?! Everything that doesn't allow that to be your reality, will you uncreate and destroy that please? Right and Wrong, Good and Bad, All Nine, POD and POC, Shorts, Boys and Beyonds.™ Thank you.

ᕉ ᕉ ᕉ

What if Six-Year-Olds Were Running the World?

When I see a six-year-old trip while walking along, they don't judge it. They don't think how wrong they were to trip. They just go, *"Oh boy, did I trip!"*

Living a conscious life means living more like a six-year-old. It's choosing for the choice that will make you joyful, not choosing for the choice that makes you feel heavy. People seem to have this point of view that living a life of consciousness is really heavy and serious, tough and difficult. No! It's the only place you actually have a life of ease and joy, whatever comes up.

I know there are people who would hear this and say—*You're just shirking your responsibility*. But I am not advocating not taking care of what needs to be taken care of. I AM ADVOCATING TAKING CARE OF IT ALL WITH A LOT MORE EASE—AND TAKING CARE OF YOU, TOO—WITH EASE.

Consciousness is pragmatic!

It includes everything and judges nothing. It includes paying your rent, and calling your parents. You may have things that have to be handled—what if you could just handle them all with total ease and be grateful for you being able to handle them?

What if you were just grateful for every time you tripped? What if you were grateful for every time you were willing to get up and get moving again, too?

Now please know that about 52 percent(ish) of the population isn't looking for anything different. They are hard-pressed to even change their underwear. They have decided they have the right answer.

It's not up to you to change anybody—it's up to them.

You can only facilitate change for someone who is willing to actually ask you a question that allows a door to open, so you can facilitate some change.

Until then, there is no change to be facilitated.

Stop trying to change people that truly don't desire change. Stop judging you for not being able to change them. It's just THEIR CHOICE to not change.

It's NOT YOUR FAULT. To repeat: it's just THEIR CHOICE. It's NOT YOUR FAULT.

The greatest gift you can give someone is to empower them to CHOOSE—even if their choice isn't working out well for them. Because then they will have the gift of their choice for the rest of their lives.

People are committed to being serious. They believe that that's more real than the space of being a six-year-old like me. People are committed to finding the perfect relationship that's going to save them and make their life perfect. People are so committed to the way things have always been instead of considering a different possibility. People are committed to always having to have the right answer. Even when that answer is dead wrong for them.

The difficulty is that the people that desire change, have in essence decided that the slim majority that don't desire change have the right answer. If you've ever gone into competition, thinking, *"I've got to get my piece of this particular pie,"* or, *"They're getting it all, and I'm getting nothing,"* then you know what I'm talking about.

Yet, when you get clear on what's true for YOU, 99% of the time, you don't care about that particular pie, nor what anyone else is getting. You were just aligning and agreeing with the points of view around you. Right now, there is only a very small percentage of people that truly desire massive change. Let's say it's 5% of the population.

Don't get me wrong, out of 6.6 billion people, that's still a lot of people.

A lot of people.

You, choosing to read this book, are one of them.

Are you willing to know that?

Consciousness Always Desires More of Itself

Expressed another way, *"Consciousness begets consciousness."* Given the chance, consciousness will always create more of itself.

Consciousness is the easiest energetic state to maintain according to the laws of physics. Why? *Because there is no polarity to keep in existence. It is the is-ness that just is.*

Let's say unconsciousness would be like a fixed point of view. Do you know people with a fixed point of view? Now, to have that fixed point of view, does it take a lot of energy to hold onto it?

Take a staunch conservative, a staunch liberal, or a fascist … they have fixed points of view that require huge amounts of energy to hold them in place, right?

It is that level of energy you have to put into every fixed point of view you have in order to keep it fixed.

For each judgment it takes 25 judgments to hold it in place. For each of those 25 it takes another 25, and for each of those 25 it takes another 25. It is the ultimate multi-level marketing program for crap.

The thing about consciousness is that it is literally the easiest state in which to be because you don't have to do the multi-level-marketing program of crap.

So, sweet, sweet being reading this ... *You have a choice* ... You could use your energy to hold fixed points of view and judgments in place—or you can use that energy to generate your life. *Your living. It's your choice.*

All the fixed points of view, projections, expectations, separations, judgments and rejections that you have of you and about you will you destroy and uncreate all those please? Right and Wrong, Good and Bad, POD and POC, All Nine, Shorts, Boys and Beyonds.™ Thank you.

Being

Magic

The Universe is Trying to Gift to You!

Imagine having these two little chubby angels flying right above you. You know, like those on the ceiling of the Sistine Chapel, flapping their little wings like crazy because they're holding a pot with gold coins in it, and it's really tough for them to stay up because this gold weighs so much....

They have so much for you that they just want to give you ... and they want to give it to you ... and they want to give it to you ... and they want to give it to you ... and they keep wanting to give it to you ... and they keep wanting to give it to you....

So, my friend, why do they keep DESIRING to give it to you instead of just giving to you?

Because you never ask for it!

They're up there going—*Come on stupid! You're testing the limits of my allowance, I'm so going to drop this on your head and kill you right now! Please ask a question that allows us to give this to you!*

Please ask. For whatever you desire. The Universe's greatest wish is that you would but ask—and receive.

(Apparently, it likes you more than you do.)

— Chapter 12 —
Wands Out! You are Magic!

You as a being—when you're truly being you—create magic! And, truth. You know that, don't you?

Situations that are supposed to turn out one way, turn out totally differently when you're willing to be that certain energy that changes every situation. Is that cause and effect, or is that magic?

It's interesting that you ALWAYS have the choice to be it, but you're only willing to choose to be it sometimes.

Make no mistake—it's a choice. It's always a choice. So what do I mean when I talk about magic? Well, from my point of view—asking for something and being able to receive it is magic. Being able to change something is magic. Just being able to change the way your life feels for example, is a brilliant bit of magic that most people don't know exists....

"Oh, You Can't Do That!"

My friend, Gary, used to tell this story about when he was a little kid. He would get out of his body, walk up on the ceiling, stick his head out the door energetically and listen to the radio programs that his parents were listening to or watch the television they were watching.

He just did that. He got out of his body and did that until one day he told his mom. Oh, big mistake!

She said, *"Oh, you can't do that!"* And he could never do it again.

That's how this reality works. This reality is like his mother was to him. This reality is like most of our mothers and our fathers. It's there to tell us what we can't do—not what we can do.

Get this! This is the key: You can create great things from beyond this reality if you are willing to be functional in and through this reality, but not owned by it.

How many times in the past did you actually create something that was magical and tell someone else about it, and they said, "You can't do that!?" Or they instantly went into judgment to find out how and why you couldn't have been able to do that....

At which point you probably decided, *"I can't do that anymore."*

See, magic is actually what you already be, it's not even something you do. It's something that you as a being have as a natural capacity, and it's something you as a being are as an expression in the world. It usually shows up when you don't think about it too much, right? When we are willing to be aware of possibilities that are greater than this linear reality tells us—beyond the cause and effect universe.

Funny enough, this "ask and you shall receive" thing really works well when we get out of our minds, when we stop trying so hard—and when we're not in judgment.

If you're doing judgment you're not doing magic. If you're doing judgment, you're not being magic. Judgment is one of the biggest killers of the magic possibility we can be.

So all the magic you made the mistake of telling someone else about, that because they didn't understand it or went into judgment about it and you could perceive it energetically, you decided you couldn't do it anymore and that it probably wasn't really magic in the first place, will you uncreate and destroy all of that now please? And be the magic you truly be? Right and Wrong, Good and Bad, POD and POC, All Nine, Shorts, Boys and Beyonds.™ Thank you.

ᘐᘐᘐ

What if You Looked at Magic as the Lightness of Being That You Are?

Think back, in the past year are there three times where you were the lightness of being that you actually are, even when it seemed like you weren't supposed to be? And did you notice the situations you were in changed around you—and got easier? That's magic. That's choosing YOUR REALITY, which is the beginning of being the magic you truly be.

Would you be willing to take the time to write three of those times down here? You can write them on another piece of paper if you like. If you get on a roll, please list as many of those situations as you can. Don't stop until you've written down as many as you can recall.

1. _____

2. _____

3. _____

As an example, there was a lady whose flights were being cancelled because they were closing Chicago airport, and she was headed to Montreal to attend a class I was giving. Let's call her Susan. So Susan asked—"*What magic can I be that will change this situation?*"

A magic tool—ask a question.

She goes to the airport, and she asks the people at the front desk: "*Is there anything you can do?*"—and the airport lady says, "*No, there's nothing we can do.*"

Susan says, "*Really? Are you sure? How does it get any better than this?*"

The airport lady sort of softens. So Susan asks again: "*How does it get any better than this?*"

The lady says, "*Uh ... well let me check.*"

Susan answers with a question, "*Thank you so much, how does it get any better than that? Thank you for checking for me.*"

So the airport lady types furiously on her computer and looks up and says, "*Wait a minute, I didn't even realize that flight was there. We have a flight that will go through someplace else and you'll actually get in 2 hours early, is that okay?*"

Susan answers with a question again, "*Oh yes, that will be just fine, thank you so much, how does it get any better than that?*"

The reservationist says, "*Oh! Apparently coach is pretty close to full, but wow, apparently there's a seat available right now in business class. Is that okay that I upgrade you for free?*"

That is magic. And, it's a true story.

How does it get any better than that?

So the first tool for you is asking: *"What magic can I be that would change this situation?"*

If you never ask a question, you don't change anything. You don't step into being the magic nearly as easily as you can, because you're not asking for something different to show up than what's right in front of you.

Remember, ask and you shall receive. Don't ask, and you probably won't receive anything different than what you're already getting. Asking a question is always the first way to change everything—a question is one of the essential parts in inviting magic into your life.

Now I know that sounds really simple—a question, great, thanks, where's the profound nature of that? Sometimes the simplest things are the most profound. Most of us learned long ago to stop asking questions. So now, we eliminate the possibilities that are available beyond this current reality.

❧ ❧ ❧

Walking down the Hallway

I mentioned this before … And it is worth repeating:

When you're functioning from answer or conclusion, it's like you're walking down a very, very long hallway, and you've decided this is where I'm going, and that is it! There are no doors. And the non-existing doors are all locked. And you left the key behind. On purpose. We are so cute!

So with the lady and the flights, where she was going to was arriving very late to Montreal—as in not getting there until the next morning. That's where she was headed. And if she had never asked a question, she would have been headed in that direction, and that's where she would have ended up.

That's what most of us do.

We're headed in this direction, and that's where we're going to end up. When you ask a question, instead of going down this hallway with walls on either side of you, doors open on all sides, with light and space behind them.

Suddenly there are possibilities that you never saw before you asked the question! How does it get any better than that? Or any easier?

The question is one key for magic to occur! That is how we allow the Universe to point out the magic that it's trying to give us!

ꙩ ꙩ ꙩ

Would You Be Willing to Be a Different Vibration?

The only thing that keeps you from magic is your refusal to believe that it exists.

Oh, and everything you aligned and agreed with and resisted and reacted to about this reality being true.

And the paradigm of cause and effect being true.

And all those limitations you picked up along the way being true.

Once you get that out of the way, magic is all you're going to have! How does it get any better than that? That's the basics of it. *So what is the crux?*

We're living on a planet where roughly 6.5 billion people do not believe in magic. For many of you reading this book—for large parts of your lives at least—this has been your point of view too, my friend. You've entrained to that point of view. Over and over again. This reality tells you: *Ticktock. Ticktock. Magic doesn't really exist.*

Entrainment is where things vibrate similarly; they start to "dance to the same drummer" so to speak. It's like putting pendulum clocks in the same room. Eventually all the pendulums will ticktock at the same rate.

Notice when you're around somebody who's really sad, and you start to become sad? And you can't seem to find your reality of happiness that you know should be there? That's also entrainment. If you listen to the drone of this reality, it's something like, *"Ticktock. Ticktock. Magic doesn't really exist."* So what does it do to you when you entrain to the vibration of the no-magic of this reality? It makes you function as though magic doesn't exist—and you can't even seem to find the reality of magic that is YOU underneath it all. *(Ticktock. Ticktock. Magic doesn't really exist.)*

How many times do you, in an effort to connect with people who aren't happy, who aren't joyful, who don't have any magic, try to vibrate like them? Would you be willing to uncreate and destroy all of that now? Right and Wrong, Good and Bad, POD and POC, All Nine, Shorts, Boys and Beyonds.™

If you're going to do (and be) magic, here's the thing—you have to be willing to vibrate beyond those who don't know magic exists and who don't believe in it.

You have to be willing to vibrate at a different rate. As in, *"Ticktock. Ticktock. MAGIC EXISTS! AND I AM IT!"*

Whether or not you entrain to someone else is your choice.

It's a choice—always. So when you notice yourself going down the rabbit hole of their reality, try asking this question:

If I were being the magic I truly be what different reality could I choose right now? Everything that stops that, would you be willing to uncreate and destroy all of that now? Right and Wrong, Good and Bad, POD and POC, All Nine, Shorts, Boys and Beyonds.™ Thank You.

Ticktock. Ticktock. MAGIC EXISTS! AND YOU ARE IT!

Illusion or Magic?

Once when I was doing a class in Rome, Italy, somebody asked the woman translating, *"Is Dain an illusionist?"* She answered, *"No dear, he is not an illusionist, he is a magician!"* The person said, *"What do you mean?"*

She answered, *"An illusionist is somebody who tries to make you think something is happening, a magician is someone who actually does it and makes magic (and change) occur."*

How many times have you believed that you're an illusionist, believing that you're somehow perpetrating this grand illusion on everyone, that you're not really the magic that you think you should be? Would you be willing to uncreate and destroy all of that now? Right and Wrong, Good and Bad, POD and POC, All Nine, Shorts, Boys and Beyonds.™

I see people who come to my classes and literally have their point of view about everything change in hours or days.

Or, they receive the change they have been waiting for seemingly their whole life—or billions of lives.

And some of them then believe somehow, *"Oh, it's just an illusion. The old stuff will come back soon."*

<u>*What if the idea that the change you created is an illusion is actually the lie that's sticking you?*</u>

That consciousness is an illusion, that you are an illusion and that you're an illusion if you're using any of these tools in this book and actually having any change, that it's just illusionary, it's not real....

What if ALL OF THAT is the lie?

You being more of you, you becoming more conscious, and more aware, and having more willingness and capacity to choose. That works. It actually works. The you that you are, when you just be you, (as though that's an easy thing—it's one of the most interestingly challenging and easy concepts that there is) and when you're that, you are the embodiment-of-magic walking.

What's the value of refusing to be the walking embodiment of magic you and your body truly be? Will you now uncreate and destroy all of that now please? Right and Wrong, Good and Bad, POD and POC, All Nine, Shorts, Boys and Beyonds.™ Thank you.

⁂

Changing What Already Occurred

Let me give you an example. My friend, Gary, and I were walking down the street in Auckland, New Zealand, a couple of years ago. They drive on the wrong side of the road there ... Wrong for me, that is. They drive on the left side of the road.

We are crossing the street, and I look left like I would do at home. No car. I go to step off the curb, and here's a car—20 feet away— it's coming from the right at about 25 miles per hour (40 kph), and my foot is on the street already, and here it comes.

Gary goes, *"No!"*

All of a sudden my foot is back on the curb, the car has moved back 15 feet and then it goes on by. Gary totally changed what transpired. I probably would have ignored it except another friend was there, and she said, *"What happened?"*

Then we both turned to Gary and asked, *"What happened? Did you do something?"*

He just said, *"Yes, I wasn't going to let you die."*

We all have this ability. I would not be talking about it if we did not all have it someway somehow. Call me weird. But I know you have this ability, too.

Please look over your life and see where you changed something that already appeared to occur or something that did not make any sense that you should be able to change.

Would you be willing to write ONE THING down? Just one. Acknowledging it. To you.

_____

_____

_____

_____

That's magic! And yes, it REALLY HAPPENED! Are you willing to acknowledge that you did that now? Please.

That's part of claiming the magic you truly be. It's the very beginning of being able to choose to generate and create more of it in the future.

Why is it that we only allow that kind of magic to happen in an emergency? How many times have you been about to die somehow, and all of a sudden something is rearranged, and you're not dead?

Have you had that? And you only allow that to occur in an emergency? It should be something you can activate by choice any moment you choose it!

Anytime!

Ticktock. Ticktock. MAGIC EXISTS! AND YOU ARE IT!

There Is No How

If you are willing to be that energy of potency and magic, you can change anything. For what reason does it have to be difficult? What if you allowed it to just occur? What if you allowed magic to show up all the time, just because you could?

It is something you can do; it is something you can be.

It's part of the energy that you as a being have access to. What is required of you is stepping out of your fixed points of view and stepping into the awareness of the capacities you as a Being truly have—even when they go beyond this reality. And the reason I'm giving you these stories as examples, is so that you know that magic exists.

There is no "how" I can use to explain that to you.

It isn't a how.

It's a that. That you can, too. That this is YOU … who you truly be. Acknowledging that opens the door.

How many lifetimes, how many hundreds or billions or trillions of years have you spent searching for the how as in the technique—and how many groups have you been a part of, or founded, or written the books for, trying to find the "how" to something that you already were?

It's not about a how. It is about being. You. Now.

Ticktock. Ticktock. MAGIC EXISTS! AND YOU ARE IT!

Being a Contribution

Let me give you another example. A man—let's call him Grant—who had been coming to my classes for several years on and off, gave me a call a few years ago.

He said, *"Hey, I'm not coming to this class—but I need your help on something."*

I said, *"OK, cool, what is it?"*

Grant said, *"I've got this little niece, and she's been born prematurely. Is there anything you can suggest that I do for her?"*

I said, *"You've been doing a lot of Access classes, you've done a lot of the hands-on body processes and received a lot of it. If you can, just touch her, and ask her to take anything from your body that she needs, whether she wants to heal her body or if she wants to get out of it. And tell her, either way, it's her choice and it's totally okay."*

Now I didn't know what impact these few words had for a long time. The next time I saw Grant, over a year later, he came over and gave me the warmest hug I've ever had from him—warmer and with more gratitude and more presence than I can even put into words.

It turned out that Grant had been present when his daughter had a miscarriage. They opened her up and all this blood came out along with this tiny little baby. This little baby was black and dead, and she was only the size of the palm of his hand.

He asked the mother and the doctors if he could hold her. He told her what I had suggested, giving her the choice to stay or go, letting her know that he would love her and be grateful for her regardless of her choice, and offering that she could use anything from his body and he knew in order to make the choice that worked for her.

He had the tools and the awareness to allow her to make a choice to live. And he was able to be there for her in a way that no one else in his family would have been able to be. He quite literally gave that little girl "access" to her life.

That is magic.

He said because of what I had told him, and that he chose to do it, and because of what he had learned from Access classes, his granddaughter is now a thriving child and "just has more life than anyone" he has ever known. The gratitude he had was palpable.

めろ めろ めろ

Now, My Friend, Please Ask Yourself:

Is there an impact you're being in the world around you that is far greater than you're actually able to acknowledge right now? And is it even greater when you—even if it is just for some seconds say, *"Screw the rules of this reality. I'm having my reality now."*

Why? Because in those 10 seconds you are willing to be magic.

Imagine if you stretched that 10 seconds into your whole life and were willing to have your reality and your awareness every 10 seconds of every day. What could you generate? What could we generate together if we were all willing to be that magic, that potent, that aware, that present and that energetically intense? What could we all generate if you stepped into that level of presence and went **Bam!?**

That is actually who you be—and it's this phenomenal gift to you and everyone around you! It's as though we've been sitting around waiting to somehow be what we consider large enough or great enough to see ourselves as a contribution, rather than recognizing that we are a contribution right now.

Right now.

Ticktock. Ticktock. MAGIC EXISTS! AND YOU ARE IT! NOW.

You think, *"Someday I'll get to be the contribution, but I'm not that today."*

So everywhere you decided that you'd be a contribution someday, and that you're not today, will you uncreate and destroy that now, please? Right and Wrong, Good and Bad, POD and POC, All Nine, Shorts, Boys and Beyonds.™

What if you're a far greater contribution than you could ever acknowledge because it doesn't match the definitive, linear reality you've made more real than the magic you truly are?

What if you being the magic you be is exactly the contribution that the world requires?

Right now.
Bam!

Ticktock. Ticktock.

MAGIC EXISTS! AND YOU ARE IT!

WILL YOU CHOOSE TO BE IT?

Stop!

Some of you went into your head and tried to figure this out.
Really, this is not figure-out-able.

I know, you have this thing called a mind, and it is useful at some points.
But this, my friend, you can't figure out with your cognitive mind. It is
beyond that.

Really, if you could figure your life out with your mind, wouldn't you have
done so already?

Everything is the opposite of what it appears to be.
Nothing is the opposite of what it appears to be.

Really.

Diary of Magic

What if you acknowledged every time you're being magic? Instead of saying that it was a coincidence, sheer luck or a fluke? REALLY acknowledged it.

To you and the Universe.

Would you be willing to start a Diary of The Magic Me?

It can be a very expensive, beautiful, hand-bound book, a piece of crappy scrap paper, a Notes page in your iPhone®, a page on Facebook® or anything in between. It doesn't matter!

What matters is that for a week, a month, a year—or the rest of your life—you'll write down every little bit of magic that finds its way into your life.

And after acknowledging that it was magic, you say THANK YOU and ask the questions: *"What will it take for more of that to show up in my life?"* and *"How does it get any better than this?"*

When we acknowledge and are grateful for things in our life, we're telling the Universe that we would like more of that. We're giving it energy. We're working with the chubby angels.

(They're very happy about that, by the way.)

This

——— Earth ———

----------- **TOOL** -----------

When you wake up tomorrow, please ask:

Earth, What Do You Require of Me Today?

Earth, what do you require of me today?

Do you require me to be more pathetic?
Or maybe you require me to hate myself more today?
Oh, of course, you require me to have some big trauma and drama and tears to prove that I am alive?

I am sorry, my friend: You're probably not going to get ANY of those answers ...
But don't listen to me. Try it out yourself. Just ask. *Earth, what do you require of me?*

Then....

Shut up!

And listen....

∽

∽

∽

There!

You perceived something, didn't you?

That's the energy of the Earth communicating with you, giving you the awareness you asked for.

Did it make you smile to ask and receive from the Earth? Was it enjoyable to take a moment of silence basking in the energy of this beautiful planet? Did you notice more ease, more peace, more space, more joy? Just asking and listening and being present creates that.

If you enjoyed it, definitely don't do it again tomorrow—or the day after that!

You are absolutely NOT allowed to do this again tomorrow and for the next 21 days after that to change your life and that of the planet.

That, too, was a joke. :)

Chapter 13

Does the Planet Really Need Saving?

I may seem really annoying to you for the next few minutes, okay?

See, I'm getting to the point where either we change, or it's not worth it. We have this beautiful, amazing, grand, glorious, phenomenal planet upon which we live. What if we actually started to acknowledge that?

We either change how we function, or the planet … won't be able to sustain life. I'd rather not have that happen. That's just my point of view. My point of view doesn't have to be yours.

What if You Are the Difference and Change This Planet Requires?

And it is fine if you don't know how to get there, or how to choose something different. You're not supposed to have the answers. What I would request of you is to please begin to *ask questions* like....

What else is possible?
What else can we create and generate?

What other energies might be available that I have never even considered?

What if being and changing isn't a linear construct?

What if you didn't have to go to A–Z and that was the end? What if you went from A to Z and noticed, *"Oh my God, there's like a billion more A's possible? Then if we had a B, that creates a whole other billion A's, plus a B combination, which is totally different than 50 A's, and then what if we added in C's? Oh my goodness, there's a billion C's too!"*

How does it get any better than that? **Maybe we are infinite? Maybe there are infinite possibilities?**

And maybe, if we acknowledge that, we could keep playing on this planet? It is a possibility!

✺ ✺ ✺

The Earth and Us

One thing you might want to look at is this: in the last 2,000 years the Earth has gone through less geologic change than at any other time in its history. Why? **Because of us.** We've had homes and things we didn't want destroyed and beautiful places. So we demanded, *"Hey Earth, could you please not destroy my house?"*

And the Earth answered, *"Sure, no problem."* Except what have we been giving the Earth in return for its kindness? Loads and loads of garbage in the form of anger, rage, fury and hate, judgment, trauma and drama, love of separation.

We never ask a question and receive its awareness and answer. For example, a good question in Los Angeles all the way through San Francisco might be, *"Earth, if we put several hundred billion tons of concrete on an earthquake fault will that be a problem for you?"*

But we refuse to ask questions of the Earth, and we refuse to listen to this beautiful planet's awareness! One of the biggest reasons is that we validate other people's realities of separation as real and true. In other words, because other people don't believe the Earth has consciousness and awareness, we don't allow ourselves to believe it either.

There are 6.5 billion people on this planet ... How many of them are choosing happiness? Almost none. How many of you reading this book actually choose happiness? Truth? For most people, hardly ever.

How do I know? Two reasons. First, because I used to be one of them. Second, because I work with people day in and day out, and when they have the option of going to trauma and drama, they often choose it—until they realize that there is a different choice. Choosing trauma and drama is not the way it has to be—*it's just the way we learned it had to be!*

So what if you were willing to give up what you learned had to be, in favor of what could be? What if you were willing to stop validating the limitation you see all around you and consider other possibilities instead? What if you knew there was something completely different possible?

And, the big question: *Is that actually why you're reading this book now?*

∽ ∽ ∽

Killing Energy

Are you aware that right now the Earth could kill every person it wanted to? How many natural disasters have you seen in the last several years? Is it decreasing or increasing? Killing energy. The earth is willing to have it. How did we get so lucky it doesn't use it on us very often?

Please know, the Earth doesn't use its killing energy just because it can … If that were the case, probably none of us would be here. *The Earth does it to facilitate consciousness.* That's why the Earth is doing what it's doing. All the time. Would you be willing to look at that possibility? That the Earth is facilitating consciousness with everything it chooses.

So everything you've done to have a point of view of "disasters" being a wrongness, will you give that up now? Would you be willing to be aware of it without having to do anything about it? My friends, I am inviting you to a completely different way of looking at the world.

What if you can walk through the world and see war and famine and go, *"OK, this is happening. What are the possibilities here?"* What can I be to contribute to changing this? And really BE THAT ENERGY, be that question, with total allowance, no point of view or investment in the war and famine being right or wrong, good or bad. What would be possible then?

You stepping out of the polarity of this reality … into the Oneness of Being.

Truth, would that change the world?

∽ ∽ ∽

Greatest Toxic Waste

What if our anger, rage, fury and hate, judgment and our love of trauma and drama and separation are the greatest toxic wastes on the planet? And if it is, it's the toxic waste we could most easily change—if we choose to. But ONLY if we choose to.

There have been numerous studies done proving that when you direct anger and judgment at a plant you kill it. This information should not be surprising to anyone. It disrupts the plant's necessary energy field to such a degree that it ceases to be able to maintain life.

Well, what does it do to the Earth to have 6.5 billion of us choosing to use anger, rage, judgment, wrongness and separation as our primary mode of functioning in our lives and with each other?

If we want to change the world, we need to stop our reliance on such harsh, outdated modes of beingness. Unless we start asking some different questions, we don't have a chance to fundamentally change the way we function in this reality and the way we function on this planet with each other.

So what's the antidote to the anger, rage, fury and hate, judgment, separation and trauma and drama?

Consciousness. Question. Choice. And Possibility.

And the willingness to change and eliminate the separation that you believe defines you. All it does, my beautiful friend, is limit you and the possibilities you have of being you, and changing the world.

So everything you've done to enforce the lie that anger, hate, judgment, separation, trauma and drama are what you'd truly like to choose … and everything you've done to buy that you have no other choice, will you please destroy and uncreate all that now? Right and Wrong, Good and Bad, POD and POC, All Nine, Shorts, Boys and Beyonds.™

୬ ୬ ୬

Does the Planet Really Need Saving?

It's funny when people talk about saving the planet. The planet does not need saving. It is the people living on it that need saving if they are going to survive.

My question is, would you be willing to facilitate the Earth?

With whatever energy it requires? Even if that may mean giving the Earth the energy it needs so enough of us can wake up? Scientists studying the global effects of the tsunami in 2003 that killed hundreds of thousands of people found that the tsunami also created a wobble in the Earth's axis so that things could not be the same anymore. Ever. A similar, but different, wobble was reported after the Fukushima earthquake in Japan in 2011.

Things had to change. Interesting.

Please know, it is actually <u>a choice to not be conscious and not be aware. Just as it is a choice to be conscious and to be aware.</u>

In the tsunami, the animals—even the animals that had been staked in the ground for 30 years—pulled up their stakes and went for higher ground. The dogs, the cats, the cows, the birds … every single animal left if it could.

And the humans went to the beach to collect fish and photograph that weird wave coming in. …

So how would you like to function in life?

Do you want to photograph—or better yet, videotape—your own death? Do you want to be taken away by a tsunami because you were too unconscious? *Or do you actually want to be aware enough to perceive the feather touch on your cheek when it is time to get the hell out of Dodge©?*

Everything that doesn't allow you to have the awareness of how to be the contribution the Earth requires … and everything that makes you think you are weird if you even consider it, will you destroy and uncreate it all please? Right and Wrong, Good and Bad, POD and POC, All Nine, Shorts, Boys and Beyonds.™ Thank you.

Are You the 100th Monkey?

Have you heard of the 100th Monkey Phenomenon? Some scientists were doing a study of some monkeys on several islands. The monkeys were separated by water and they didn't swim from island to island.

Because the monkeys were running out of food, the scientists started to drop food there from planes. They would drop crates from planes, the crates would open from impact, and the monkeys would eat the food, even though it was often dirty.

Then one day, one monkey not bound by the limits of then-current reality, started to wash the dropped food. So, one monkey would do it and then teach another monkey, and then teach another monkey.

As soon as 100 monkeys, confined to one island, actually got this thing of washing their food, all the monkeys—on all of the islands—started washing all of their food, without having been taught, or told by any learning mechanism we've been taught to acknowledge.

Why?
They changed tracks.
There was a critical mass of consciousness, so to speak, that became available to every monkey connected to that network of monkeys, and reality changed for all of them—simultaneously.

They changed the consciousness of all of the monkeys by having enough monkeys, having enough awareness and enough consciousness of what would be better for all of them. *What if that's the possibility for how change can occur for us, too?*

What does it require? Well, cognitively you have no clue. Because it's not a cognitive process. And it's not linear.

What if something COMPLETELY different is possible?

For all of us? With all of us. Together?

That's why I talk of ending our insistence on buying—and functioning according to—the rules of this reality: because doing so has created the seemingly impossible mess we are currently in. We require something different.

Now.
Are you ready, monkey?

—————————— TOOL ——————————

Do You Feel Angry Yet?

Good.

Here is a thing you have to know about anger.

Anger is often potency (power) you are suppressing.

In other words, anger and potency (power) feel exactly the same.

They *"feel"* exactly the same.

You won't be the potency of you because you have always misidentified it as anger.

Why do I use the word "potency" instead of power? Because power as it's commonly identified and used in this reality means "power over another." **Potency, on the other hand, is your capacity to choose and create a change.**

Every time you were a little kid and you went, *"You know what, this has got to change!"* your parents and teachers went, *"Don't be such an angry little kid."* And there you were, stuck with the point of view that, *"This is bad, and I shouldn't do it, and I shouldn't be it, and I can't do it and can't be it."*

What if even as a little kid, that anger was actually POTENCY? Just look at it for a second: when you get to a point in your life and KNOW that this has to change—is that anger or is that potency?

And is that where you are right now in this 10 seconds?

HOW DO YOU KNOW?

(Here is the tool.)

You ask a question, my dear friends. (Surprise?)

The question is: *"Is this anger or potency?"*

Whatever is light to you—that is what it is.

Then you know. And you can choose what to be and do from that space consciously.

Bring Everything On!

Has anyone ever said this to you?

"You have too much going on!
Why don't you ever focus?"

Focus? Calm down? One thing at a time?

Is that really light for you?
Is that true for you?

Could I possibly invite you to look at it from a
completely different angle?

You are **supposed to and entrained** to desire to do as little
as possible. The ideal in this reality is when you finally have
enough money that you don't have to do anything anymore.

Here is my question to you: **Wouldn't you be bored?**

You have capacities beyond your wildest dreams, my friend.

Play with them!

How many of you bought the lie that you desire to do less, not more, and
that you're more you when you have less to do? Would you be willing to
uncreate and destroy all of that now? Right and Wrong, Good and Bad,
POD and POC, All Nine, Shorts, Boys and Beyonds.™ Thank you.

What if you actually chose to live exuberantly instead of just
having a life counting down to death? What if you chose to
play, create, generate, have fun, enjoy your body and experience
the world fully and totally all the time?

What if that is the space where you're at peace?

What if INTENSELY LIVING is restful for you?

What if you're really only truly happy when you have at least 5 (to 25) things you are working on at all times??? And what if it weren't a wrongness any longer?

Kingdom

of Being

The Back Doors

How many of you have not truly acknowledged that your job here is to facilitate consciousness and change? How many back doors do you have wide open so that you can escape? So that you don't ever have to truly choose it? Or you?

Most people don't even know what consciousness is.

They believe that if their eyes are open they are conscious.

Would you be willing to acknowledge that you have no clue what it is either? And that you also know what it is in totality? Will you now make the demand that you will perceive, know, be and receive exactly what consciousness truly is—and exactly what it demands of you?

Everything that stops that, will you uncreate and destroy all of that now, please? Right and Wrong, Good and Bad, POD and POC, All Nine, Shorts, Boys and Beyonds.™ Thank you.

You can let the back doors be there, if you like. Consciousness includes everything, also back doors. But what if you let your awareness perceive the doors of possibilities THAT ARE YOU? In totality?

And open them.

What if you being you **IS** changing the world?

Right now.

In this 10 seconds.

— Chapter 14 —

The Kingdom of We

I know, we've talked about choice already ... And you really don't like doing things twice do you, my friend? This is Choice, Part 2. The sequel about the Kingdom of We.

Have you noticed that just the word CHOICE makes some people cringe? *I can't choose. I don't want to choose. Why do I have to choose? Please, please, please choose for me!* Weirdly enough, most people don't understand what choice truly is.

Yet, the willingness to choose is the beginning to committing to your own life. Being you and changing the world is something you—**choose**.

You have choice. You always have choice.

One of the things we try to do is believe we are alone in our own universe. As though we're alone, and in our own kingdom, and that is it, and we can choose only for us. Or that if we're choosing for something that works for somebody else, too, then we're choosing against us, and we believe that the only way to choose for us is to choose against somebody else.

What if you were more like an animal? One of the things about animals is, they have an instinct for what is survival—not just for them—but for the entire planet and everything on it. They don't just function from survival, contrary to popular belief, but THRIVAL. For example, when rabbits know it's going to be a drought the next year, they highly diminish their breeding. And they normally breed like ... bunnies! Does this contribute to just them—or to everyone?

When humans are aware that they are not able to sustain their population based on water in a particular area, what do they do? They build MORE HOUSES! When they are having a tough time financially, or in their relationships, what do they do? They have more babies! Is this insane to anyone else? What if we were to take a lesson from the bunnies? And the horses? And every other animal on the planet?

We try to believe that we are all alone, and we have to choose only for us. Otherwise, we're not choosing for us, we're choosing against us. What if that were another one of those BIG LIES that you've bought? What if, when choosing consciously, it actually included you and the entire planet and everyone on it? And what if what was rewarding would be rewarding for you and everyone else?

You can either create the kingdom of me (aloneness) or the kingdom of We (Oneness).

Which would you rather choose?

✑ ✑ ✑

You're Well Connected

You've been sold that you need to be alone in order to choose for you. But once you try to create that aloneness, you can't make a truly conscious choice ... **Could an infinite being ever truly be alone? No!**

Weird, eh? You're infinite. You're connected with everyone and everything.

The moment you try to create the lie of aloneness, you separate yourself from everything that would allow you to make a choice that would be rewarding for you and everyone. In other words, in order to try to buy that lie that you have to be alone in order to choose for you, you cut yourself off from all the awareness you could have that would allow you to make a choice that would go in the direction you want.

You cut yourself off from the caring that you have for you and for other people. For you, that caring has to be a factor in all of your choices. When you try to choose only for you, you also cut yourself off from the potency you have by virtue of your connection to other people and their awareness and their caring and contribution.

You cut yourself off from everything that makes you the brilliance of you in order to go into this artificial lack of space you create that you think is the only place from which you can choose.

Now.

I am inviting you to choice that doesn't start from the perspective of other people's limitations or your limitations. It's functioning from choice that actually does include everyone and everything, but isn't limited by it and isn't limited by other people's judgments.

It's being embraced by the oneness that is the universe, the gifting that the sun and the planets and all animals, the plants and the trees are to you—that the universe is to you. And that you are to it.

Would you be willing to choose by including the entirety of the consciousness of the world that desires to gift to you in your choices? Will you now uncreate and destroy everything that doesn't allow all of that, please? Right and Wrong, Good and Bad, POD and POC, All Nine, Shorts, Boys and Beyonds.™ Thank you.

So what is it that you actually know that you've been pretending not to know or denying that you know that if you allowed yourself to know it would allow you to have the total choice for oneness in every moment of every situation?

Will you now uncreate and destroy everything that doesn't allow all of that, please? Right and Wrong, Good and Bad, POD and POC, All Nine, Shorts, Boys and Beyonds.™

∾ ∾ ∾

Exclusion Is Not Oneness

Are you aware that you've actually been refusing a kingdom of oneness (the Kingdom of We)? And when I say oneness, there's all kinds of things you've done in other lifetimes, all kinds of spiritual things where the idea was, *"Oh, let's go off, and we'll create a cult together, and it will be oneness."*

Except that's not oneness, because you're having to go off into the forest somewhere, and there may be 50 or 100 or 200 of you that are supposedly trying to create oneness—by yourselves. That's not oneness.

Oneness is the inclusion of <u>everyone</u> and <u>everything</u> with absolutely <u>no judgment.</u>

In those lifetimes you so wanted to deny your knowing, you so wanted to believe in what everybody else was telling you, because you knew somewhere oneness should actually exist, but you denied your knowing in order to have somebody else's point of view about what that should be. So you followed that person, and when it didn't turn out well you declared, *"Oneness must not really exist. I'm never going to do this ever again!"*

You put yourself into resistance and reaction at that point and now when anything says its oneness you think, *"No way, I'm not doing that again, they got me last time."*

I would like you to follow your knowing.

I'd like you to follow your knowing without judgment, however. Most people on the planet have no idea what knowing is because they always think it's *conclusion*.

✐ ✐ ✐

Conclusion as the Litmus Test

It's the biggest thing that sticks you regarding choice—you think that choice is actually coming to conclusion, but it's not. Every time you come to a conclusion about anything you cut off your awareness of everything that's not that conclusion. Would you like that again in English?

When you conclude, that conclusion becomes the answer, the right stopping point, against which all subsequent input (either from awareness or conclusion) is measured. That conclusion becomes the litmus test everything else must match. And if it doesn't match the conclusion, you throw it out.

I get it! (Unfortunately, from a lot of personal experience doing exactly that.) We're pretty much doing this all the time ... How are we going to stop it?

The answer to that is—CHOOSE TO STOP. Choose to do something different.

As a result of that simple choice, you're going to go through your life, and you're going to choose something based on the old paradigm, and for just a moment, you're going to have this stutter, and you're going, *"Wait, wait, wait, wait a minute, hold on, I don't have to do that—do I?"*

That's going to be the beginning of freedom for you. The freedom to choose something completely different.

I once had a woman who had come to me for a session telling me that she had set up her whole life so that she wouldn't have to choose. Even continuing at a job she didn't like was a way of avoiding having to choose. Ever. She said, *"I'm too scared to choose a career that puts me in the position to have to choose for me every day."*

Notice what this is truly about—setting up structure in life so she didn't have to choose any longer. I'm sure you've never done that, right? Of course not! But just in case: *How many structures have you set up in your life to eliminate choice? Everything that is, will you uncreate and destroy all of that please? Right and Wrong, Good and Bad, POD and POC, All Nine, Shorts, Boys and Beyonds.™ Thank you.*

∽ ∽ ∽

If You Had Total Choice Available, What Would You Create?

Everybody is choosing all the time. Everybody's choosing their life and their living. Consciously or not.

When a new possibility came up, you could choose to have the limited perspective of, *"Oh my God, this is a terrible thing, and I'm going to die ..."* Or you could actually choose to have this other perspective I'm talking about which is, *"Wow, I wonder what else we can all create now?"*

What if you were willing to create the kingdom of We—which includes all of us but doesn't include our limited points of view as relevance, just awareness?

What if with all the limited points of view you're aware of with the people around you, what if you were just aware of them? What if those limited points of view didn't have to enter into the choices that you made as a relevance?

What if limited points of view had no relevance to you? If you had total choice available and you were choosing to generate the kingdom of We, what would you choose? Everything that doesn't allow that to show up, will you destroy and uncreate all that please? Right and Wrong, Good and Bad, POD and POC, All Nine, Shorts, Boys and Beyonds.™

If you ask this question and function from this question, you're not going to look at your interactions with people from the place of, *"Oh, I need to separate from them and choose for me!"* or *"I need to choose for them and separate from me!"* which have been most people's only two choices. Instead it's going to be from a different place that includes us all.

It's up to all of us to create this kingdom of We.

And if enough of us do, we will create that as a possibility in the world. Something completely different!

Are you ready? What do you choose?

Am I Choosing or Concluding?

Remember we talked about the difference between a judgment and an awareness? Awareness has no emotional charge on it, and you are willing to give it up and change it at any time.

Now, many people confuse CHOICE with *deciding* or *concluding*.

They are completely different things!

But how do you know? How do you know you're actually choosing something—not deciding or concluding that this is what you have to be, do or have?

Again—it is the lack of charge and the movement of the energy.

When you choose, there is no charge to it. You choose—and if required, you choose something different in 10 seconds, without judging the choice or you. You're willing to be aware of and follow the energy wherever it's required.

Choice is never final. Choice is a continuous process. You choose and then you choose again. And again. And again.

Or, as a teenager in one of my classes so brilliantly summed up:
"Choice is cool! Conclusion sucks!"

Your Point of View Creates Your Reality

Are you a problem solver? A really good one, even?

Congratulations!

How many times have you tried to solve the problem
of getting this reality right?

Then you do! For 10 glorious seconds you have absolutely no problems.

And then somehow a new one appears.

**When you are a problem solver, you always, always,
ALWAYS have to create new problems to solve.**

Now look at the world.

If we see a world full of problems, what world are we creating?

If we instead choose to see EVERYTHING, with no judgment—a world
full of possibilities—what world would we be creating?

Just ponder that. And know this.

*Your point of view creates your reality;
reality does not create your point of view.*

What points of view would you like to choose?

Leading

Without Followers

Would You Be Late for Your Own Party?

Have you bought the lie that it is too late? Too late to change everything here that you know needs to change because it is not working for any of us?

Really, my friend, would you plan a party—the biggest party of all our lives—and then get the date wrong?

I don't think so. Even you, the screwed up humanoid you are, would not plan a party for that long and get the date wrong.

If it were too late, you would not be here right now!

You would have come much sooner to change things, because you know—and have known for 4 trillion years—exactly when the pivotal time would be to awaken consciousness and awareness.

So wherever you bought the lie that it is too late and you can't be enough and you might as well give up now, will you please uncreate and destroy all of that? Right and Wrong, Good and Bad, POD and POC, All Nine, Shorts, Boys and Beyonds.™ *Thank you.*

Please know—you picked the planet, and you picked the time. You knew it and still do.

We're right on time.

(And, as you always do, you have, of course, waited until the very last moment possible, so get to work!)

— Chapter 15 —
Are You Willing to Be a Leader?

I look at being a leader from a totally different place than most people. From my point of view, being a leader is when you're able to know what you know and follow what you know regardless of whether anybody else goes along. It doesn't exclude anyone, because anyone can come along—IF THEY CHOOSE IT.

That's what being a leader is from my point of view.

In this reality to be a leader you must have followers. I totally disagree. My point of view is that in order to be a leader you must lead yourself, and if anybody else follows because you've got such a brilliant idea, no problem. But if you're truly being a leader you will empower them to know what they know, not simply get them to try to follow you.

This is a totally different concept in leadership. For me, that's what's required if we're going to change tracks on the planet right now. Being a leader is being willing to step into what you know and follow it. It's really that simple. It's about having a sense of trust in you and your knowing, even when that knowing doesn't match other people's points of view.

The Four-Minute Mile

Let me give you an example—nowadays its very common that competitive male runners will run a mile in under four minutes. In fact, if you don't run a mile in under four minutes you can't even be considered a college-class runner anymore, let alone a world-class athlete.

Except for a long, long, long, long time—thousands of years—well okay, let's say a thousand years from the time that they started being able to keep time, there was no such thing as a four-minute mile. It was considered an impossible barrier to break through.

Until one day, one guy went, *"You know what, I can do it!"* Literally, all of his friends and all the people around him were saying, *"You can't do that, nobody can do a four-minute mile!"* Yet his point of view was, *"Yes, I can!"*

"No, you can't. There's no way. You'll never do it," the people around him would say.

He said, *"Watch me!"*

And he did. In 1954, Roger Bannister broke the four-minute barrier. Since then, once everyone saw it was possible, now everyone runs less than a four-minute mile. Now it's like, *"Okay, can we get down into the 3:55's, down to the 3:45's, can we get down to the 3:40's?"* So there's been a totally different standard that's been created by one person being willing to be a leader.

What if you knew that even in the smallest choices of your life that you can be exactly that contribution to people?

A Day Without Judgment

Let's say you've got people around you that are in huge amounts of judgment of the rightness or the wrongness of some political philosophy. And you know you could judge it as right or wrong or you could just see it as somebody else's interesting point of view.

What?

Well ... when you judge something as right or when you judge it as wrong, you actually contribute to it being in existence, and give it more energy, and make it more solid, and make it less able to change.

What if we could come out of the necessity of having the rightness of our point of view and the wrongness of anybody else's and instead realize that we all have points of view and that some of those points of view that other people have—that we may not even like right now—might actually also contribute to changing the planet?

What if one step to becoming a leader were about getting out of judgment? From my point of view, consciousness is where everything exists and nothing is judged. Where you could have anything be exactly as it is and not have to judge it in any way.

Can you imagine if you woke up and had no judgment in your head and no judgment as you went throughout your day at all, no matter what you did? What would that day be like? *Can you imagine a day with no judgment?*

You know what—it's possible, we just haven't been taught to embrace it. We haven't been entrained to view it as a valuable product. If enough of us could come out of judgment and demand that "no matter what it takes, I am not going to be judgmental anymore," the world would change that very day. Would you be willing? Now?

Asking for Change

Let me summarize ... The first part of being a conscious leader is trusting you and following your knowing. The second part is coming out of judgment of you or anyone or anything else. Because then you can truly be present for everything with no point of view....

The third part is begin to ask questions in your life. So, how does that work?

Let's say you see something like the Gulf oil spill occur in 2010. What I heard from a lot of people was, *"It's such a devastation, it's such a terrible thing, it's such a devastation, it's such a terrible thing, it's such a devastation, it's such a terrible thing...."*

What I would ask the people that were open enough to hear it is was, *"Okay, so are you aware that by continually having that point of view you create it as more devastation? Because your energy, your fixed point of view goes into creating that."*

It's like what science tells us—when we observe a molecule, we change it. The reason we change it is because we have a point of view that we impose on it! What if we could be in such no judgment and no fixed point of view that we could observe that molecule and invite it to change rather than impelling the point of view that it must change to match our conclusion?

What if we could be in such a connection with the molecules around us because we had no judgment that we could invite them to change at will also?

The next thing I asked was, *"Would you like to change it?"* They looked at me like I had hit them over the head with a sledgehammer, *"What do you mean, change it?"*

I said well, why don't you just do this one thing, ask this one question, *"What would it take to change this? What would it take to undo the ecological devastation?"* So they would look at me like, *"Oh my God, I never thought of that. I was just lamenting the fact that it was such a problem."*

What would it be like if, for anything we wanted to change, that the beginning point of that change was simply asking a question?

In Access, we kept asking that question, *"Can we do anything about the Gulf today? Is there anything we can contribute today?"* It took 2½ months of asking every morning, *"Is there anything we can do to change this? Is there anything we can do to change this?"* We kept getting a no. Then on one day we got a yes. That was apparently the day they capped the well.

So we sent out an email to all the people in Access Consciousness and at a particular time on a particular day, we asked them to contribute their <u>energy</u> to changing the ecological devastation in the Gulf. Three days later, in an article on July 27th in the *New York Times*, it said scientists were amazed at how quickly the oil was disappearing.

On August 4th the *New York Times* had an article saying most of the oil had been dissipating and that which was left posed far less of a threat to the ecology and the ecosystem than they would have ever thought possible.

This was a place we could all put our energy that had no judgment, that had total question, as in, *"We don't know what can happen, but let's do something, and let's use the potency that we have available."* Please note, the only thing we asked for was change in the ecological devastation. Not what it would look like.

Now, was that just all of us in Access Consciousness that changed it? Maybe. But you know what? Maybe it was everyone who had a desire to change that possibility in the Gulf and who had the point of view that it was possible?

The important part is not WHO changed it, but that it changed—and that, together, we have that capacity. Maybe it was the bacteria that went, *"Hey, we can help here,"*—like the animals coming to the rescue in the movie *Avatar*. The exciting part is that level of change is possible! It's not only possible, it happened!

Three-Headed You

Now, my friend, if you said, *"Hey, you know what? I'm going to contribute energy to changing the oil spill in the Gulf!"* would people around you applaud? Or shake their heads?

They would probably look at you like you had three heads and came from Mars, right? They would look at you like you were a nut-case and needed to be locked up right now. How many of you have felt that way most of your life? Have you ever wondered, *"Why do people keep looking at me like I have three heads?"*

Because to them you do!

Because you want something different than what they want—you actually desire change. Which is why it's so necessary that if you're going to create that change, you have to be willing to step up to being the leader you are that you haven't been willing to be. You receive them looking at you like you have three heads. You receive their judgments and their idea that it's impossible to change. And then, you go and contribute to the change anyway.

That's being a leader.

❧ ❧ ❧

Walk Your Talk

You have to BE IT. Not show it. Or try to share it. When you share, you have to go down to their size to try to bring them up to your size. Except, they are never your size, because by definition, you are going down to their size to create a commonality, which will allow you to have a connection.

Really simply: SHARE means SHRINK!

DEMONSTRATE what is possible instead.

Is everybody going to choose to be what you demonstrate it is possible to be? No. And <u>some</u> people will see it as a possibility—then choose to become some of it. Or all of it, as they choose. You are demonstrating what is possible. They can step into it or not. It does not affect you anymore.

What's required now is people who actually take the baby steps into consciousness right now and show other people that it can be done. It's the choices you make that open up more consciousness for you—and for all of us.

You'll look at something that you thought had to be a certain, limited way in the past, and you'll see a different possibility, and you'll choose it! You'll see how that affects your life and how that choice occurred for you, and that's exactly the information people require that they don't currently have. But you look and say, *"I'm just living my life. Nobody would be interested in hearing about this."*

You are actually incorrect. The people around you that desire consciousness are very interested in hearing about that, even if they don't know they're seeking more awareness. You are already being this phenomenal gift— and yet so few of us are willing to acknowledge ourselves as the leaders of consciousness we truly be. It's far easier and far more rewarding than you think!

You're some of the only people on the planet that actually desire to change what's going on! And you're the only person in your life that is actually able to generate, create and institute what it is you would like in your life.

If you can't honor you enough to be that for you, how can you create what you would like in life? You will always have to stop anything that would create judgment or create you being judgable—or an enemy—in someone else's universe.

Let me give you two different possibilities for navigating the minefield called this reality:

1. You keep doing the tip-toe thing in life, trying to avoid stepping on a mine of someone else's making, avoiding making enemies, succumbing to other people's limited points of view, and then BOOOM, you step in the wrong place, and you get blown up ... painfully over and over again ... every time you try to tip-toe around the judgments of others....

2. Now, imagine there's another way you can be in the world, where you're saying, *"Oh, a mine!"* and you gladly step on it <u>if it's time for it to be stepped on</u>. As it explodes around you, you're simply noticing, *"Wow, that was kind of loud and intensely cool. How does it get any better than that?"*

And you're not blown up, and you're not destroyed, and you actually walk through life stepping on any mine that requires being stepped on to change the face of the planet. If that mine is going to facilitate consciousness, you step on it! And so be it!

You become the energy of being that does not make an apology for itself.

It's like, *"Here I am."*

Everything that doesn't allow that to show up, will you destroy and uncreate it please? Right and Wrong, Good and Bad, POD and POC, All Nine, Shorts, Boys, and Beyonds.™ *Thank you.*

∽ ∽ ∽

Claiming the Potency of You

About a year after I started Access, Gary Douglas asked me if I was willing to claim the potency of me. At that moment, I was standing behind this wall partition where we were ... I stuck my head out, I wouldn't even go and face him totally.

And I said, *"Well, what will that mean?"*

He said, *"I can't tell you."*

I stuck my head around the wall, *"What will it look like?"*

"I can't tell you."

"What will happen?"

"I can't tell you that either. You are just going to have to claim it if you are willing to have it."

It literally took me about 45 minutes of "hemming and hawing," wondering if I could choose it if I didn't know what it would look like, and thinking the whole time, *"What would happen if I did?"*

And then I did. I chose to claim my potency. It was like, *"Here's what's actually true, and I'm not going to continue lying to myself anymore. I'm going to be whatever is actually true for me, because you know what, my living is too valuable to me to hide anymore."*

I chose to be a leader. I continue to. Every ten seconds. I am not looking for followers. I am just willing to be the invitation to something completely different.

Are you?

Is now the time?

If it is, you know it. And if not, that's perfectly OK, too.

So now the question: "Will YOU now claim and own and be the potency and consciousness you truly be?"

If so, everything that doesn't allow that to show up with total ease, will you destroy and uncreate it and let us change it together on 3? 1 ... 2 ... 3! Right and Wrong, Good and Bad, POD and POC, All Nine, Shorts, Boys, and Beyonds.™ Thank you.

What if there was a living possible that was beyond anything that any of us have ever imagined?

What if what the Earth requires of us is to let go of all our self-imposed limitation and instead embrace the magic we truly be?

What can you choose that will create the result YOU desire to create in the world?

Everything that doesn't allow that to show up, will you destroy and uncreate it all please? Right and Wrong, Good and Bad, POD and POC, All Nine, Shorts, Boys, and Beyonds.™ *Thank you.*

What Else Can I Add to My Life?

You've read the first 15 chapters of this book.
How does it get even better than that?

Now.

Check, please. Is this light to you?

I can hear your heads spinning.
What if you didn't come to conclusion, but instead went to question?

Remember, this book is not a book of answers.
It is a book of questions.

What if there were no right and wrong?

What if you didn't have to make any of what you are reading in this book right in order to receive whatever part of it might work for you?

And what if you didn't have to make any of what you learned in the past wrong in order to receive what I am inviting you to?

What if you could keep all you knew and just add the new things that worked for you?

What if your point of view could be:

"What else can I add to my life?"

Thank You, for You

Take a moment to notice You.

Here you are, reading the last pages of this book.

Being you.

Would you be willing to be grateful for you—right now?
Being grateful for whatever this moment brings, wherever you are,
whom you are with and what sweet body you have.

Isn't that what you have been looking for your whole life?

I am sure you have read many books before this one. Books about
spirituality, about how to trust yourself, how to be a better person, how to
get the purple light to do spirals of love while you stand on your head and
sing hallelujah ... (Well, maybe not the last one.)

But isn't this what you have been looking for—to be grateful for your life
and grateful for you and grateful to be alive?

If there were one really big key to the kingdom, this would be the one . . . .

Gratitude.

So, for just ten seconds, would you be willing to simply bathe
in gratitude for you and your body? Let it be all around you, in
you, over you under you—like an infinite embrace.

Total gratitude. What would that be like in your body? What possibilities for living would open up? What would gratitude invite into your living?

Gratitude. All the time. For you and your body.

I will tell you a secret later.

Now please bathe.

✑

✑

✑

Ok, it is now later.

The secret is that when you have gratitude for you, you can't help but have gratitude for everyone else.

It is just there.

You be it. Gratitude.

The End ... and

Beginning

Celebrating the Stuck-Ness

Please know, after reading this book there is another way of Being that you are going to become aware of.

Now and then you may feel like you're stuck.

That it is the time to celebrate!

Because what you are becoming aware of is that the stuck-ness you've always *thought* was you—isn't.

You are getting the awareness that the stuck place is DIFFERENT from you. It isn't you anymore! That's precisely why you can perceive it— because you are coming out of being it.

You are on the verge of going from the resisting and reacting of, *"How to undo everything to have anything?"*—to *"What would I like to be, do, have, create and generate now beyond all of this?"*

You're about to take off. So celebrate that you can perceive the stuck-ness so clearly now—it shows you what to let go of that isn't you.

My dear friend, lift your feet and learn to fly.

Now is the time.

— Chapter 16 —
The Beginning

This is almost the end of the book—and the beginning of something completely different. If you choose it. Please know, no one can choose for you. You are the creator of your life. The only thing standing in the way of you is … You.

We've looked at many areas in this book. And we've cleared much of what may have been standing in the way of you stepping into Being You.

Your awareness has increased, whether you know it cognitively or not. Your potency has increased, whether you know it cognitively or not. Your capacity to receive has increased, whether you know it cognitively or not.

If you allow it, it will continue to do so. If you ask for it. And use the tools you have so generously put in your path.

And make no mistake about it … It is a process.

It is BEING YOU, CHANGING THE WORLD.

The energy keeps moving and shifting and changing—it is continuous: Being. What you were 10 seconds ago, is no longer. You are a new you. And it is continuous; changing. What was required for you to change when you started to read this book may not even be relevant anymore.

When I tell the story of how Access Consciousness saved and changed my whole life, some people think it was all done there and then, way back in 2000. Let me tell you—the process is still on! I joyfully, curiously, excitedly and out of necessity use the tools I've introduced you to in this book every day! Almost every moment of the day.

Sometimes I get really uncomfortable. I feel stuck. I go into the wrongness of me. The difference is that where before it would take months or weeks or days to get out of it, it can now take an hour, or even minutes. By asking questions. By using the tools (like questions and POD POC). By receiving from the universe. By choosing something different.

Today I view every little bit of sweet stuck-ness as a gift—although sometimes grudgingly so. It is another layer of this reality popping up to be cleared and changed.

But more importantly, I use the tools to generate and create the change I'd like to see in the world—and the life I desire! You can do that, too. These tools are meant to be used. A lot. They don't wear out. They are easy. They are yours! There is no need for any guru—except you. With these tools you can be the master of your universe. And there are a lot more tools available beyond this book.

The areas of being we've looked at in this book—the judgment, body, sex, relationship, receiving, caring, abuse, family, magic, choice, leadership—are areas that repeatedly come up in my classes. I use these very tools to facilitate change in people's whole universes. The ones whose lives truly change, are the ones that go home and keep using the tools, keep stepping into the energy of Being (whatever that looks like for them) and keep asking the questions.

Since I was a child, all I wanted to do was change the world. My greatest joy is hearing how different people's lives are after a class—and how that change continues to grow. How their bodies no longer choose to hurt. The ease they're having with themselves. What difference they are able to be with their children and loved ones. The contribution they are to the people around them. The potency they're stepping into in the world.

Sometimes a previous brick-hugger comes up after class and gives me a hug from a place of such vulnerability and receiving that we both just melt into tears and oneness. How did I get so lucky to be a contribution to change? I am more grateful than I could ever express in words.

In all these areas, my own living and being is something completely different than it was eleven years ago, and five years ago, and three years ago—and one year ago. Yet, I keep looking, I keep asking—in total amazed gratitude for what I've received and generated—what else is possible here? What can I generate and create differently that I haven't yet acknowledged? And what can WE?

It is the greatest adventure I could ever think of inviting you to: *The exploration of Consciousness: Being You, Changing the World—and Beyond.*

Most modalities you've come into contact with, spiritual and otherwise, will show you how to fit better into this reality. How to function, benefit, win and not lose based on what everyone agrees are the rules and regulation of existing. Access is different. Completely different. It shows you how to go beyond this reality.

So Here Are Your Marching Orders, My Friend.

You are a gift, the likes of which the world has never seen before.

It's irrelevant who you thought you were before you got here. You are you, something far greater than anyone has ever seen. Now is the time.

∽ ∽ ∽

You can fight it, you can hide from it, but you'll never again be able to avoid it.

Even if the world never changed, don't you know you have a different life to live?

Now is the time.

Anything you ever felt left out of, you are not left out of this.

You've been demanding change, while refusing it just as much, so you take tiny steps forward instead of quantum leaps.

Now is the time for a difference.

∽ ∽ ∽

Everything you thought was you is not enough.

You are far greater than anything you could think.

You're an energy of being that has never been seen before.

Now's the time to be it, to embody it, to receive the possibilities that go beyond this reality.

To step into such allowance of you and everything, such potency, such joy, that you become the difference the world has been asking for.

Now is the time.

⁓ ⁓ ⁓

We have an Earth around us that is getting sicker. We have a world that needs us. Not just our families, not just our friends, not just our city, state or country—the world requires what we know.

What we each know, that we've been hiding from everyone, including us.

Now is the time for your knowing to awaken. For your knowing that goes beyond what this reality is—to the being that you know is possible.

Now is the time where we unlock the knowing that you've hidden from everyone, including you. Now is the time where we unlock the consciousness of you as you truly be.

⁓ ⁓ ⁓

You knew we would get to this point and this moment and this day. You knew.

Will you acknowledge that?

You knew the time would come to step into being the acoustic you.

The being that is beyond definition and beyond judgment, beyond caring about the limited points of view of this reality.

The being you've done your best to hide from for four trillion years.

Now is the time, and we are the keys.

Let us unlock everything that would allow you to now Be.

What if being were something totally different than anyone has ever decided it would be?

What if you could let go of your definition of self, your definition of separation, your definition of judgment and everything that defines you as less than the oneness you be?

∽ ∽ ∽

How many of you know you want just a slightly better version of this reality? What if that were not enough for you?

What if you know EVERYTHING has to change?

But what if it were easy and spacious? What if it were not change as this reality tells you is necessary? What if it were change from a totally different place?

What do you know that you've been pretending not to know for a very long time?

What are you that you've been pretending not to be for a very long time? Are you willing to know it and be it now?

Because, my friend, it takes all of us.

∽ ∽ ∽

We all have the stories of our lives, the reason we can and cannot choose from our justified point of view....

What if that were all crap?

What if we created a totally different source for reality? What if you know what that is, have known what it is for a very, very, very long time?

Now is the time to re-awaken it.

Here we are together again, different bodies, different creations that we call our lives. Here we are together again to change.

To create change. To generate it and institute it. Something we do very, very well.

Now is the time to unlock the doors you personally came here to unlock. Now is the time to unlock the doors together that we came here to unlock, whatever they be.

Now is the time to open the door to being totally acoustic. To acknowledge our capacity, our ability and that our very being is the destruction of everything limited.

Now is the time.

❧ ❧ ❧

You have far too much joy to bring the world to allow yourself to be mired in the sadness … And if you haven't known it, it's only because you've perceived so much of the sadness the world around you chooses.

It's only because the world around you makes the sadness more real than the joy you know is possible. And it's only because you've hidden it underneath mountains of other people's realities, believing that if you allowed it to be seen it could be crushed or destroyed.

But nothing anything or anyone has ever done could truly destroy it, because you are here right now.

Now is the time to awaken that joy. We require it, the Earth requires it, the universe requires it and begs us to have the courage to open up that difference called joy that we be.

Now is the time.

What change will the Earth request of us?

Step into all the potency you've ever mustered or considered possible and then go beyond it and gift change to the Earth for whatever it requires because it, as you, knows.

Are you willing to step into being the tsunami of consciousness? An acoustic wave that changes everything in its path?

That goes wherever it chooses, knows exactly where it must go and doesn't allow anyone or anything to stop it.

Ever again.

Now is the time.

✐ ✐ ✐

Time for the gentle potency we be, the intensity of potency that we be, the difference called potency that we be, that is the change the world has been asking for.

You are that which allows consciousness to be.

You knew and asked that this demand be made on you. In fact, it's a demand that you placed on yourself, a request and an insistence.

Now is the time, as you have requested.

Allow everything you know to come into being.

My friend, I don't necessarily know what it is that exists in a completely different world.

I just know it is completely different.

Welcome to your completely different world.

Epilogue

Who You Be?

1. Think of someone whose energy was similar to yours before you started to read this book.

Someone you would have said, "Oh, they're just like me."

Pick up the energy of that person now.

Do you perceive them differently?

Are you different?

2. Think of someone you feel at ease with.

Someone who doesn't judge you (too much) and totally cares about you.

Now ———————————————— see yourself through their eyes.

What do you perceive differently?

3. Would you be willing to be that person?

Would be you be willing to be at ease with you, not judge you, and totally care for you?

Now ———————————————— be with you.

Who you be?

Explanation of the Access Clearing Statement

The clearing statement we use in Access Consciousness is:

Right and Wrong, Good and Bad, POC, POD, All Nine, Shorts, Boys and Beyonds.

Right and Wrong, Good and Bad
Is shorthand for:
What's good, perfect and correct about this?
What's wrong, mean, vicious, terrible, bad and awful about this?
What's right and wrong, good and bad?

POC
Is the point of creation of the thoughts, feelings and emotions immediately preceding whatever you decided.

POD
Is the point of destruction immediately following whatever you decided. It's like pulling the bottom card out of a house of cards. The whole thing falls down.

All Nine
Stands for nine layers of crap that were taken out. You know that somewhere in those nine layers, there's got to be a pony because you couldn't put that much crap in one place without having a pony in there. It's crap that you're generating yourself, which is the bad part.

Shorts
Is the short version of: What's meaningful about this? What's meaningless about this? What's the punishment for this? What's the reward for this?

Boys

Stands for nucleated spheres. **Have you ever been told you have to peel the layers of the onion to get to the core of an issue?** Well, this is it—except it's not an onion. It's an energetic structure that looks like one. These are pre-verbal. Have you ever seen one of those kids' bubble pipes? Blow here, and you create a mass of bubbles? As you pop one, it fills back in. Basically, these have to do with those areas of our life where we've tried to change something continuously with no effect. This is what keeps something repeating ad infinitum....

Beyonds

Are feelings or sensations you get that stop your heart, stop your breath, or stop your willingness to look at possibilities. It's like when your business is in the red, and you get another final notice, and you say argh! You weren't expecting that right now.

Sometimes we just say, "POD and POC it."

෴ ෴ ෴

For a more in-depth explanation of the clearing statement, with video and audio, please visit drdainheer.com.

About the Author

Dr. Dain Heer

International speaker and author, Dr. Dain Heer travels all over the world facilitating advanced classes on Access Consciousness. He invites and inspires people to more consciousness from total allowance, caring, humor and a phenomenal knowing.

Dr. Heer started work as a Network Chiropractor back in 2000 in California, USA. Having worked with bodies since he was in college, Dr. Heer came across Access Consciousness at a point in his life when he was deeply unhappy and even planning suicide. Access Consciousness changed all of that. When none of the other modalities and techniques Dr. Heer had been studying were giving him lasting results or change, with Access Consciousness, his life began to expand and grow with more ease and speed than even he could have imagined possible.

Today Dain is best known for his powerful energetic transformation process, called The Energetic Synthesis of Being™ and for being the co-creator of Access Consciousness, along with the founder, Gary Douglas. Dr. Heer has a completely different approach to healing by teaching people to tap into and recognize their own abilities and knowing. The energetic transformation possible is fast—and truly dynamic.

Dr. Heer hosts a regular radio show entitled Conversations in Consciousness, appears on *Dr. Pat, VoiceAmerica* and has been a guest of multiple radio shows. He has been featured on the cover of *Insight Magazine* and has appeared on several TV shows, including *Good Morning* show in New Zealand, *The Circle* and *Morning Show* Australia.

Dr. Heer is the author of eight books on the topics of embodiment, healing, money and relationships. His latest book, *Being You, Changing the World,* was first published in June 2011. It has been translated into Swedish, German, Spanish, Italian and Estonian and will be released in French, Japanese, Polish and Slovenian during 2016.

About Access Consciousness

Access Consciousness is available in 173 countries and has contributed to changing the lives of more than 30 thousand people around the world for the past 25 years. Delivered through seminars, teleseries, books, audios and consultations, what most people love about it is that it actually works!

Access Consciousness is an ever-evolving energy transformation program which offers you the tools and questions to create everything you desire in a different and easier way and to change the things in your life that you haven't been able to change until now. Access is based on the idea that you're not wrong, that you know and that consciousness can shift anything. It provides you with ways to become totally aware and to begin to function as the conscious being you truly are. It gives you access to the possibilities that exist when you no longer stick yourself and no longer believe that you are stuck. If you had total choice available, what would you create?

- *If your purpose in life were to have fun, what would you change?*
- *If you were celebrating your life today, what would you choose?*
- *What else is possible that you've never considered?*

The aim of Access Consciousness is to create a world of consciousness and oneness. Consciousness includes everything and judges nothing. Consciousness is the ability to be present in your life in every moment, without judgment of you or anyone else. It is the ability to receive everything, reject nothing, and create everything you desire in life—greater than what you currently have, and more than what you can imagine.

The information, tools and techniques presented in this book are just a small taste of what Access Consciousness has to offer. There is a whole Universe of processes and classes. Although these tools have generated a great deal of change in the lives of many people, Access Consciousness does not declare itself to be the only way. Access empowers you to know what is true for you. It allows you to know that you know!

If there are places where you can't get things in your life to work the way you know they ought to, then you might be interested in attending an Access Consciousness class, workshop or locating a facilitator. They can work with you to give you greater clarity about issues you haven't yet overcome.

Explore more at: www.accessconsciousness.com or www.drdainheer.com.

Access Seminars, Workshops & Classes

If you liked what you read in this book and are interested in attending Access seminars, workshops or classes, here is a quick sample a taste of what is available.

A Taste of Being
Facilitated exclusively by Dr. Dain Heer

During this evening you get to explore what is possible in the three signature classes Being You Changing the World, Energetic Synthesis of Being™ (ESB) and Symphony of Possibilities.

In addition to the tools of Access Consciousness®, Dain Heer uses elements of his unique energetic transformation process the Energetic Synthesis of Being. By working on one person in the room, he is inviting everyone to the change that is truly possible.

Prerequisites: None

The Being You, Changing the World Event
Facilitated exclusively by Dr. Dain Heer

Are you always looking for that "something" we all know is possible? What if that "something" is YOU? What if you being you is all it takes to change everything?

This 3½-day class is built on the pragmatic tools and perspectives presented in Dr. Dain Heer's book *Being You, Changing the World*. It is for the seekers of the world, for the people in this world that know there is a different possibility. That not only know it, but know they should be able to have it. What if the only thing keeping you from having the life you truly desire, are the tools and inspiration to create it?

Each class is uniquely created by the people who choose to come; together, we'll go on a journey of creation to a space that has never existed before. You're offered dynamic tools to assist you in changing any area of your life and an up-close experience of the unique transformational energy process the ESB while Dain works simultaneously on everybody in class to create a space that allows the change you are asking for to be.

You are invited to a different possibility. You are invited to the adventure of Being You, Changing the World.

Prerequisites: None

Access Bars®

Facilitated by Access Consciousness Certified Bars Facilitators worldwide
In this one-day class you will learn the Access Bars, a hands-on energetic process and the very foundation of Access Consciousness®.

You have 32 "bars" of energy that run through and around your head. They store the electromagnetic component of all your thoughts, ideas, attitudes, decisions and beliefs. Touch one bar and you begin to clear away the energy locked up in that aspect of your life and open up for receiving. This way you can clear limitations in areas like money, aging, body, sexuality, joy, sadness, healing, creativity, awareness and control, and many more. What would it be like to have more freedom in all of these areas?

The participants learn the Bars points and participate in both gifting and receiving two Bars sessions.

Prerequisites: None

Access Foundation

Facilitated by Access Consciousness Certified Facilitators worldwide
This four-day class undoes the foundation of limitation you've been thinking you have to live from as though you have no other choice!

It's an intense exploration of what else is possible and it creates awareness of the foundation of awareness that you haven't been using yet in your life. You will begin to see the points of view that limit you and what you can change that would allow you to function from question, choice, possibility, and contribution. You start becoming aware of your capacity to choose totally different things than you've been able to choose before. With ease!

The class provides hundreds of tools, including some hands-on body processes that allow you to change anything that isn't working for you in your life.

Prerequisites: Access Bars

Choice of Possibilities
Facilitated exclusively by Gary Douglas and Dr. Dain Heer

The Choice of Possibilities four-day class is where you begin to see what is actually possible for you because of the difference you are and how to be that with greater ease.

You will gain access to a space where you begin to recognize your capacities as an infinite being and how truly unique you are. You will start becoming aware of the choices that you make and what you would like to generate as your life with ease … financially, in relationships, in your work and beyond.

When you stop creating from your past you can start generating a future that is unlimited. What if sensing the possibilities could replace judgment of everywhere you are right or wrong? What else would you like to add to your life? And what catalyst for change could you be in the world if you unleashed the real you? What if you are the possibility you've been looking for?

Prerequisites: Access Bars, The Foundation

The Energetic Synthesis of Being ™ (ESB)
Facilitated exclusively by Dr. Dain Heer

This three-day class takes you deeper into the wondrous adventure of Dr. Dain Heer's Energetic Synthesis of Being (ESB)—a unique way of transforming limitations into possibilities and healing, for you, the world and the planet.

Dain works simultaneously with the beings and bodies in the class to create a space that allows the change that everyone is asking to show up. In working with one person, everyone is invited to that change. You will be introduced to a level of being and energetic awareness that goes beyond everything you've experienced before. The molecules in your body start to change—and you become aware of the catalyst you are for a different possibility in the world. The result is an acoustical wave of oneness that encompasses the present and the future.

What if you didn't have to separate anymore from anyone or anything... including you? What if you could have it all ... and all of you, starting now? What would you be able to create as your life and in the world?

Prerequisites: Access Bars, The Foundation

Access Body Class

Facilitated by Access Consciousness Certified Body Class Facilitators worldwide

The 3-day Body Class is designed to open up a dialogue and create a communion with your body that allows you to enjoy your body instead of fighting against it and abusing it. When you start to change the way you relate to your body, you start to change how you relate to everything in your life..

During this class, you will learn verbal processes and hands-on bodywork that unlock the tension, resistance, and dis-ease of the body.

Do you have a talent and ability to work with bodies that you haven't yet

unlocked? Are you a body worker (massage therapist, chiropractor, medical doctor, nurse) looking for a way to enhance the healing you can do for your clients? Come play with us and begin to explore how to communicate and relate to bodies, including yours, in a whole new way.

Prerequisites: Access Bars and The Foundation

Other Access Books

Benevolent Leadership for a Better World

In this book, you'll discover a non-conventional approach to leadership that allows you to lead your life and your business without limitation. This book challenges the traditional standards that underpin the business practices of most enterprises and offers an alternative that will allow you to become a conscious benevolent leader.

You will discover what it takes to actually create a sustainable future and sustainable reality in this time of great change. *By Chutisa and Steve Bowman and Gary M. Douglas.*

Living Beyond Distraction

When you find yourself in a situation that you don't seem to be able to change, you may be stuck in a distractor implant. Distractor implants are the reason we believe we have no choice in anything. A distractor implant is triggered by the events of your life and keep you from being all that you can truly be and having the life you would truly like to have.

This book provides information and effective tools that will enable you recognize the distractor implants and become free of them. *By Gary M. Douglas and Dr. Dain Heer.*

Beyond the Utopian Ideal

In this reality we use conceptual constructs like culture, religion, relationship, family and sexuality to create a purpose and a sense of rightness. These things are not actually real; they are conceptual realities that we buy into. We give up our awareness and accept the notion that being normal and just like everybody else is the best and only way to be.

These ideal concepts and constructs create huge limitations and barriers to what is possible for you. If you want to create a world that works for you, they have to come off. *By Gary M. Douglas.*

Money Isn't the Problem, You Are

This book is written for people who live in a constant state of difficulty around money, whether it's spending too much, not having enough, or having too much. Gary Douglas and Dain Heer share tools, and points of view that you can use to change the way money flows into your life. Douglas and Heer have helped those who had $10 in their pocket and people who had ten million. The interesting thing is they all have the same issue—and it has nothing to do with money. It has to do with what they are unwilling to receive. What you are unwilling to receive creates the limitation of what you can have. Change THAT and money isn't an issue any more! *By Gary M. Douglas and Dr. Dain Heer.*

Joy of Business

What if business is the adventure of living? What if business was joyful and fun? What if it was so much more than you ever perceived possible? If you were creating your business from the JOY of it—what would you choose? What would you change? What would you choose if you knew you could not fail? Business is JOY, it's creation, it's generative. It can be the adventure of LIVING ... *By Simone Milasas.*

Conscious Leadership

The Conscious Leadership book is a gift to every individual, leader and organization dedicated to creating a life that is greater than what they now have, and to making a difference in the world. It is an invitation for those people who choose to be more conscious in their leadership, with an emphasis that no particular way is right or wrong. *By Chutisa and Steve Bowman.*

Conscious Parents, Conscious Kids

This book is a collection of narratives from children immersed in living with conscious awareness. Wouldn't it be great if you could create the space that would allow your kids to unleash their potential and burst through the limitations that hold them back? To create the ease, joy and glory in everything they do and to consciously take charge of their own lives? *By the contribution of many authors.*

Divorceless Relationships

A Divorceless Relationship is one where you don't have to divorce any part of you in order to be in a relationship with someone else. It is a place where everyone and everything you are in a relationship with can become greater as a result of the relationship. *By Gary M. Douglas.*

Embodiment:
The Manual You Should Have Been Given When You Were Born

The information you should have been given at birth, about bodies, about being you and what is truly possible if you choose it ... What if your body were an ongoing source of joy and greatness? This book introduces you to the awareness that there really is a different choice for you—and your sweet body. *By Dr. Dain Heer.*

Magic. You Are It. Be It.

Magic is about the fun of having the things you desire. The real magic is the ability to have the joy that life can be. In this book you are presented tools and points of view that you can use to create consciousness and magic— and change your life in ways you may not even be able to imagine. *By Gary M. Douglas and Dr. Dain Heer.*

The Place, A Novel

As Jake Rayne travels through Idaho in his classic 57 Thunderbird, a devastating accident is the catalyst for a journey he isn't expecting. Alone in the deep forest, with his body battered and broken, Jake calls out for help. The help that finds him changes not only his life but his whole reality. Jake is opened up to the awareness of possibilities; possibilities that we have always known should be but have not yet shown up. *A Barnes & Noble best-seller by Gary M Douglas.*

The Ten Keys to Total Freedom

The Ten Keys to Total Freedom are a way of living that will help you expand your capacity for consciousness so that you can have greater awareness about yourself, your life, this reality and beyond. With greater awareness you can begin creating the life you've always known was possible but haven't yet achieved. If you will actually do and be these things, you will get free in every aspect of your life. *By Gary M. Douglas and Dr. Dain Heer.*

You'll find all these books and more in the Access Shop on www.accessconsciousness.com.

Some Ways to Connect with Access Online

www.AccessConsciousness.com
www.DrDainHeer.com
www.GaryMDouglas.com
www.BeingYouBook.com
www.TourOfConsciousness.com

www.YouTube.com/drdainheer
www.Facebook.com/drdainheer
www.Twitter.com/drdainheer

www.Facebook.com/accessconsciousness.com
www.YouTube.com/accessconsciousness.com
www.Twitter.com/accessconsciousness.com

An Invitation....

If you've enjoyed this book and would you to hear more from me in the future, you can also join me online.

The Being You Video Adventure

Would you like to discover more of what it means to truly be you and receive tools to create a totally new reality? Then please sign up for this free video series with a series of tools about Being You.

www.BeingYouClass.com

The Tour of Consciousness

I also have is a free on-going video-series with possibilities, inspirations and tools from traveling all over this beautiful Earth of ours. Come along; allow these video-greetings to empower you to know what you know! Sign up here: www.TourOfConsiousness.com

My gift to you!

Dain